C000120094

ARCHIVES AND THE EVENT OF GOD

McGill-Queen's Studies in the History of Ideas
Series Editor: Philip J. Cercone

ARCHIVES AND
THE EVENT OF GOD

The Impact of Michel Foucault
on Philosophical Theology

David Galston

McGill-Queen's University Press
Montreal & Kingston • London • Ithaca

© McGill-Queen's University Press 2011
ISBN 978-0-7735-3776-7

Legal deposit first quarter 2011
Bibliothèque nationale du Québec

Printed in Canada on acid-free paper that is 100% ancient forest free
(100% post-consumer recycled), processed chlorine free

This book has been published with the help of a grant from the
Canadian Federation for the Humanities and Social Sciences, through
the Aid to Scholarly Publications Programme, using funds provided
by the Social Sciences and Humanities Research Council of Canada.

McGill-Queen's University Press acknowledges the support
of the Canada Council for the Arts for our publishing program.
We also acknowledge the financial support of the Government of
Canada through the Canada Book Fund for our publishing activities.

Library and Archives Canada Cataloguing in Publication

Galston, David, 1960-
    Archives and the event of God: the impact of Michel Foucault on philosophical
    theology / David Galston.

    (McGill-Queen's studies in the history of ideas ; 51)
    Includes bibliographical references and index.
    ISBN 978-0-7735-3776-7

    1. Philosophical theology. 2. Religion–Philosophy. 3. Foucault, Michel. I. Title.
    II. Series: McGill-Queen's studies in the history of ideas; 51

BL51.G35 2010   210.1   C2010-904355-3

This book was typeset by Interscript in 10.5/13 New Baskerville.

Contents

Preface and Acknowledgments

THIS IS A PHILOSOPHICAL WORK. More accurately, it is a work in the field of philosophical hermeneutics. Drawing on the insights of Michel Foucault, particularly in *The Archaeology of Knowledge* and *Discipline and Punish*, I develop an understanding of human interpretation as an event. Only then does the question turn to the concept of God as an archive event and to a consideration of what this might mean for theological thought.

To avoid confusion or disappointment on the part of the reader, I want to stress two points. First, I am not defending or criticizing a religious tradition (Christianity in the main or any other) or asking if God as a thing or an object exists (a popular question today). The existence or nonexistence of God is irrelevant to this study. My concern is not metaphysical principles but practical experience. "God" is significant in this work not as a reality (or reality itself) but as a social effect or product.

Second, my study is not of a social scientific nature. I am not trying to use logical proofs or tested methods to make a truth claim. It would be impossible, in any case, to use the thinking of Foucault in this manner. Foucault understood truth to be a product of method: the method used to examine the outside world interprets the world according to the openings the method produces. With Foucault, truth is produced linguistically in styles, technologies, and arrangements of space. He even brought this understanding to bear upon himself, not claiming that his method was true but rather that it was a way to prod the imagination. This work shares that spirit. It is an experiment in thinking about how "truth" is produced in human experience, how indeed it is a type of experience. The task at hand, therefore, should be seen in the context of the continental tradition of philosophy rather than in the social-scientific sense of philosophy.

I want to thank McGill-Queen's University Press for accepting this project, which admittedly is not easily defined. In the course of its development, I gained much from the care and conversation of two McGill scholars, Philip Buckley and Richard Hayes (now at the University of New Mexico). Their friendship meant a great deal to me when I started the study of Foucault. Equally, there are several reviewers, who remain anonymous to me, who read the initial draft and offered valuable criticism and advice. There was much encouragement for this project, several excellent suggestions, and expressed hope that I would persevere despite needed revisions.

I also want to acknowledge the inspiration of two outstanding scholars and original thinkers who befriended me and in many matters offered sage and supporting advice, Don Cupitt and the late Robert W. Funk.

Finally, I want to thank my editor, Kate Merriman, for her hard work and assistance in trimming my sometimes strange language skills. And I want to thank Barbara Hampson, to whom this work is dedicated, for her reading of this text, her editorial suggestions, and her choice to walk this difficult path with me.

I have tried to make the presentation of this work precise and clear, but Foucault is not an easy thinker and the way I have chosen to use Foucault is not particularly easy either. Yet, however difficult the undertaking, a work must remain comprehensible. There are many who offered their time and attention to ensure such is the case, but of course failures in this regard belong to me.

ARCHIVES AND THE EVENT OF GOD

What Is Philosophical Theology?

IF ONE WERE TO CHART THE COURSE of philosophical theology, no doubt the river's current would flow through Aristotle, wind its way in and out of Thomas Aquinas, and crash on the shore of Immanuel Kant.[1] I am not proposing to write this history, but I would like to make a point.

In the Western tradition, the philosophical contemplation of theology has a long-standing tie to proofs for the existence of God and related problems (such as evil), but the "God" in question, perhaps beginning at Melitus, has consistently found its form in Aristotelian logic. Thomas Aquinas supplied the most famous summary of five ways to prove that this necessary and perfect being exists.[2] For centuries, philosophy was defined by the engagement of theology and theological metaphysics, and indeed the relationship was so close that seldom, before Kant, could philosophy and theology be separated. Even William of Occam, who pushed revelation outside the realm of reason to create two realms of inquiry, accomplished his scheme as a type of theological act to protect the freedom of God.

Only David Hume's skepticism was able to shake the foundation sufficiently to bring about a crisis. Before Hume, one was apt to believe that philosophical speculation eventually led to answers in

1 In Aristotle's *Metaphysics* the necessary being is defined as the being without potential and without imperfection (Book Theta); later, the necessary being is called "actual being" (ον ενεργεια in Book Lamda). These definitions are key to Aquinas's term, *actus purus*. When I refer to the history of philosophical theology, I am restricting my comments to the Western tradition of philosophy born in the Ionian city of Miletus and resting on the concern for ultimate reality.

2 Aquinas, *Summa Theologica* I, Q.2, Art. 3.

theology; reason finds its purpose and crown in revelation. But Kant discredited this working hypothesis when he took Hume seriously and concluded that indeed philosophical speculation does not lead anywhere but to more philosophy. It is not possible to climb the ladder of the sensible world to arrive at the knowledge of a certain, yet hidden, most perfect being. Our senses, rather, reach a limit, the limit of our own imagination trapped inside our own consciousness. We cannot leave the foundation of our "image-making" experience to arrive at an ideal form isolated from the very experience involved in idealizing that form.

Human experience is always involved in the imaging of the world, even when that image is God and even when the question is revelation. Traditional proofs for the existence of a supernatural God not only involve human experience; they cannot eclipse it. God as a noumenal reality is beyond the limits of reason, and as a phenomenal reality is unknown to reason. Although for the purposes of social order Kant sidestepped this troubling conclusion by proposing that God is a moral necessity, he remained firmly convinced that certainty about the existence of God is not available to reason.

After Kant, philosophical theology could move in two directions, each with two fault lines. One direction was positivistic philosophy with its fault lines running along the platform of logic, on the one hand, and social science on the other. On the side of logic, it remained possible to debate whether Kant had defeated the traditional arguments offered in defence of Aristotle's God or if he simply misunderstood the nature of religious language. Eventually analytic philosophy focused on religious language as a particular type of language-game: the actual existence of God is secondary to the symbolic purposes of the linguistic performance. On this foundation, religion is a form of life that one can choose to enter or ignore.

The second fault line on philosophy's positivistic side surfaces when religion is explained psychologically. This is sometimes called the "naturalistic" study of religion and it centres on the use of social scientific disciplines. One might, for example, explain the presence of religion in human experience as a primitive residue that still haunts modern perception. Though the facts of science explain most natural phenomena, demonstrate rather clearly evolutionary processes, and can incorporate chaos as a principle of creativity, all without a supernatural being, naming the world in terms of an intimate, omnipresent, and omnipotent parent who upholds a purpose and design for all that is remains psychologically part of human experience.[3] God is, then, not a natural (objective) reality but may be an unavoidable psychological reality. This latter reality, in terms of human behaviour, can be the subject of social scientific investigation.

But in addition to the positivistic approach, Kant spawned a philosophical approach to religion that can be called hermeneutical. This approach also has two main fault lines: one moved in the direction of German idealism (emerging as phenomenology and existentialism), and one turned idealism on its head to emerge in theology either as radical religious atheism or radical religious orthodoxy. On the side of phenomenology and existentialism, the task of philosophical theology is to interpret religious symbolism as dramatic expressions of history and life. God (or Being) may or may not be an actual entity, but God is the deepest structure of the human psyche. God is, in other words, the reconciliation of an individual or a nation or a people to fate. God is the full presence of history and the implicit hope that participation in history can define a purposeful life. Theology contemplated philosophically according to this approach centres on the drama of the human quest for meaning. It can be called an apologetic form of speculative theology because it affirms (defends) "God" as a deep and final reality.

The hermeneutical approach, however, can turn in a different direction according to its second fault line. Religion can be explored as a means of overthrowing false gods and liberating the human psyche from a self-deception that (ironically) includes religion. It can encourage revolution and the destruction of idols. In this way, theology can be called "radical" in taking either a negative theological (religious atheism) form or a positive theological (religious orthodoxy) form.

In the negative hermeneutical sense, theology works to undermine the constructs of God (or ultimate value or meaning) and to open the psyche to the horizon of radical freedom. Here religion is seen and affirmed as a human creation. If religion has value at all, it lies only in its ability to represent ideals that remain worthy enterprises: love, for example, or political justice, or self-acceptance. But when

---

3 The idea that religion and belief in God survive as a psychological "meme," proposed by Richard Dawkins and popularly available in his bestselling book *The God Delusion*, is indeed at one with this thinking. See *The God Delusion*, 170–217.

religion as a human creation mistakenly posits itself as yet another unapproachable ultimate, that is, when it arrogantly stands for reality in total, then it too has become both an idol of deception and one worthy of grave critique.

In the positive hermeneutical sense, theology is a symbolic enterprise that puts noumenal reality, residing beyond human experience, into conflict with the phenomenal reality of human experience. It remains an orthodox form of theology because the noumenal location of God must, to be represented phenomenologically, rely on the expression of symbolic formulas and unapproachable liturgical customs. Thus, conservative postmodern theologians such as John Milbank and Jean Luc Marion can continue thinking with very traditional notions of God that, they maintain, break in on the world as "word" and "revelation" from the outside (noumenal) realm. The radical freedom found in the negative expression of hermeneutical theology is redefined positively as the radical freedom of the divine to break in on the human world. (In essence, this is a postmodern version of Occam's nominalistic philosophy.)

There are, then, two types of philosophy of religion and two fault lines in each type (and different expressions along each line): the positivistic with its fault lines in analytic philosophy and the social sciences, and the hermeneutical with its fault lines in apologetic and radical speculative theology. When one chooses to undertake a study in philosophical theology, the question "What type of theology?" is paramount. How one approaches the subject largely determines what questions will be asked, what reasoning will be employed, and what purpose is being served. Philosophical theology is not a singular subject but rather one of avenues and choices.

This summary is not intended to do full justice to the complex, historical, and often uncomfortable relationship between philosophy and theology, but it serves to set up the context and subject of my question. I want to know what philosophical theology looks like if the thought of Michel Foucault is taken seriously. Foucault provides several new questions for the study of religion, the shape of which depends on whether one chooses the road of positivism (the analytic tradition) or hermeneutics. In part, this new potential is due to French structuralism and the unique way Foucault (who was not a "structuralist" but certainly familiar with its milieu) changed the condition of the questions posed. As when Kant took Hume seriously and claimed to have woken up, there is a type of wake-up call for theology found in Foucault. For instance, in structuralism the focus is on language and the relationship of the linguistic signifier to the signified. But Foucault and several of his contemporaries began to take one step further into "post-structuralism" or "postmodern" thought. In effect, in post-structuralism, the positivistic emphasis on language found in structuralism combines with the hermeneutical sensibilities of phenomenology to emphasize language as the producer of reality. Language does not refer to the deeply structured human psyche, as I will explain somewhat briefly in chapter 1, but creates it. Post-structuralism rests on this latter insight and in this way is both a positivistic and hermeneutical task.

Still, it remains correct to say that in Foucault language remains primarily a critical hermeneutical concern. Institutions and histories locate the functions of language as well as disseminate its power within a social setting. Even highly abstract descriptions of an object or event reflect both the location and influence of the observing eye.[4] Language cannot be separated from its embedded position in cultural history or from its capacity to define and formulate the experience of the "now." The very structure of discourse and its dispersion, according to Foucault, is already a hermeneutical event. That is, language creates (rather than identifies) a hermeneutical structure. Thus, to undertake the study of language historically, to enter its sense within a given discursive strata, to comprehend the "now" of a particular epoch, is to encounter the epistemological creations of language. Foucault called such strata or *epistemic* layers of language "archives." He examined these archives through his unique projects of archaeology and genealogy. With Foucault, entering an archive is a supremely hermeneutical act. It involves exploring physical and linguistic evidence, understanding the dispersion and recombination of linguistic events, and – the most difficult task – relating the act of seeing to the act of stating (or, as Gilles Deleuze puts it, relating "visibles" and "articulables").[5] From these meticulous and difficult studies, Foucault gained the fundamental insight that language is a

---

4 See Foucault, *The Birth of the Clinic*, especially the comments on the "medical gaze," 107–17.

5 Deleuze, *Foucault*, 47–69.

mode of production (form) and distribution (order). In short, language is power.

When this challenge is taken into philosophical theology, a key choice is made over whether one wants to stay on the positivistic side of the question – thus examining, as can be done, religion as a linguistic form of life – or to enter the hermeneutical struggle of asking how linguistic acts produce religious concepts. My choice is to engage the hermeneutical side of the question and to explore the thinking of Michel Foucault in the hermeneutical mode of theology. But caution is necessary. Some readers might regard this work as primarily positivistic and, perhaps unconsciously, relate it to questions and conclusions in that stream of thinking: that is, some may think the point is to provide a naturalistic explanation for religious feelings or theological concepts. This is not correct. True, Foucault tends to cross the line, or perhaps simply blur the line, between positivistic and hermeneutical philosophy. His questions and examples have a positivistic flare even though his intentions are hermeneutical in flavour. It is accordingly difficult to avoid the tendency to blur the same line. Still, reading this investigation as following a naturalistic line of inquiry would be a mistake. Rather, the point is to examine human experience as a hermeneutical event. Or, to put it another way, the point is to use hermeneutics against itself. This approach is very much in the spirit of Foucault. Although Foucault turns to naturalistic metaphors – language, power, institutions, modes of production, etc. – his effort essentially is to describe how language creates a hermeneutical environment and how, as such, the environment itself is a problem of hermeneutics. My attempt, which will consist of demonstrating how theology can be regarded as a type of side effect of language and power, will engage these problems not to dispel theology on naturalistic grounds but to bring to theology the hermeneutical problem of itself. Once this task is completed, the more difficult question of the future of theology opens to new horizons. While my example is specifically Christian theology, I believe the analysis can be applied generally to religion (and thus I occasionally use the two words interchangeably).

The particular setting for this enquiry is Christian systematic theology, which is the tradition in which I stand. I consider it important to state, in the age of religious extremism, that I hold no pretense that one religion is superior to another or that religion in any form is a necessary part of human life, now or in the future. However, I do wish to engage one question and one tradition seriously. That question concerns the idea of God as an effect of language and the tradition of Christian philosophical theology. I hope that some elements of this exercise will have relevance in other contexts, too.

Reviewers of this work offered several criticisms that can now be addressed. One is the location of this book in relation to the broader field of Foucault and religious studies. A second relates to the very style of this book, which raises a somewhat peculiar question and brings some unique elements of Foucault's thought to bear on philosophical theology. Since the second concern relates to the very intention of this work, I will address it first.

When Don Cupitt read through the draft of this book and offered some extremely helpful comments, he left me with one question that requires a response. Almost immediately he asked why not focus on priestly power and practices of confession? No doubt this avenue could be pursued profitably and would likely come to some of the same results that I reach in this work. But in the end I did not focus on ecclesiastical practices. Though such practices are strategies of power, formations of discourse, and distributions of force in social history, I chose not take examples from here for two reasons. One is simply that I am not a student of church history and I have little or no relationship to its various and multiple forms of organization and reasoning. Equally, one could argue that only in the Middle Ages did the church's social status enable it to be a genuine player in major strategies of power, and since the Enlightenment that power has moved definitively to the state with the church at best playing the role of its moral apologist. Today even that has changed, as Cupitt's many books indicate. In the Western experience, it is becoming increasingly difficult to define what place religion in general or the church in particular might hold in society. Indeed, Cuppit has strongly argued that it has no role anymore except to highlight and perhaps celebrate the ideals of the Enlightenment: peace, justice, and "*jetztzeit*"[6] or the immediacy of joy in life. Therefore, I did not go down the road of ecclesiastical forms of power expressed through practices of confession or the priestly office, first because my philosophical interest outweighs my historical interest, and second because I did not feel

6 Walter Benjamin's unique phrase, normally translated as "the time of the now."

these particular forms held in a sufficiently contemporary way the expression of power I was seeking to examine.

I base my understanding of power on Foucault's *Discipline and Punish* and the image of the Panopticon. Mainly, I seek to display the power/language relationship in the production of truth as well as indicate how this production has what I call side effects. The Panopticon allows for this level of examination: it focuses on the individual subject and the experience of that subject; and it exemplifies the whole social matrix or *episteme* that values a specific form of power/knowledge. Because my task is to display religious experience as a phenomenon of power and its side effects, the point is not to question the validity of religion or ask whether it can be reformed in light of contemporary knowledge (questions that Cupitt has raised successfully) but to focus on a more mundane level. How can one explain the fact that religious feelings occur in human experience? Or, how can one understand philosophically the phenomenon of theology, of systematic reflection on religion, in human experience? I think that Foucault offers some interesting ways to approach this question and that those ways are found in archaeology, genealogy, and the idea of the archive. The Panopticon seems admirably suited to unite all these concerns as well as help answer the question.

The larger question, and the first cited above, relates to how philosophical theology generally has received Foucault. This question is harder to answer since, as my opening paragraphs suggest, the answer depends on what one believes philosophical theology to be. One could argue that there has not been a reception of Michel Foucault in philosophical theology at all. Rather, Foucault has been used merely to raise various themes or tropes that might have some usefulness to the study of religion. In this regard, the question is how Foucault's understanding of religion can be raised in a religious studies context. Three works by Jeremy R. Carrette – his useful anthology that includes several selections from Foucault's works and interviews pertinent to religion, and his equally illuminating books *Foucault and Religion* and *Foucault and Theology* – are exactly about this.[7] Carrette's work is outstanding in terms of highlighting what Foucault can offer religious studies. He draws conclusions from Foucault that fit into areas of study already defined by religion and theology. But Carrette's

7 Carrette, ed., *Religion and Culture*, x; and *Foucault and Religion*.

work is limited to the nature of a commentary that seeks primarily to draw out relevant associations between Foucault and religion. It is largely descriptive of what Foucault has already said, sometimes explicitly, about religion or a religious theme. Carrette places what Foucault has said in the categories theology as a discipline has already established.

On the other hand, taking the style of Foucault into the question of religion and "thinking" religion in a Foucauldian way is a different matter. To think a question is not the same as commenting on a thinker. Using Martin Heidegger's eminent phrase, understanding a thinker is one thing, but "taking up a thinker's quest and pursuing it to the core" is quite another.[8] What I hope to accomplish is the latter. This project calls for taking up the thought of Foucault and making it work in the setting of philosophical theology. The issue of whether or not the original thought includes religious comments remains ancillary. The point is to think the question.

Where then is the "thinking" of Foucault taken up in the study of philosophical theology? Carrette and, equally, James Bernauer suggest that the answer lies in what I call negative hermeneutical theology. Foucault gives us the tools to transform religious thinking from "a discourse of religious transcendence to one of radical immanence."[9] Since Foucault focuses on discourse and power, he can draw the questions related to religion out of the sky, so to speak, and place them into the practices of daily life. One can focus on ethics, as Bernauer does, in the immediate sense of the aesthetics of the self (*parrhesia* or "speaking frankly").[10] Foucault radically critiques teleological notions that hold history under the bondage of totalizing discourses and thus delivers the human subject to a new horizon; this places the subject in the "now" and invokes a creativity of presence. Equally, with Foucault's emphasis on limits, exclusions, and boundaries, one can highlight the "outside" or "unspoken" to develop a type of noumenal (sacred and silent) relation to the "other" (outside) of history. Both acts define a "negative" form of theology: the first by the negation of traditional notions associated with a transcendental God, and the second by the

---

8 Heidegger, *What Is Called Thinking?*, 185.

9 Carrette, *Foucault and Religion*, 103. See also the foreword to this work by Bernauer and Bernauer, *Michel Foucault's Force of Flight: Toward an Ethics for Thought.*

10 Bernauer, "Confessions of the Soul," 568.

transgression of the boundaries of the self. These are indeed legitimate developments in religious thinking, and I rely on some of these
conclusions. But still, are they examples of thinking philosophical
theology by means of Foucault or of highlighting religious themes already present in Foucault? Since I place much emphasis on this distinction, it is worthy of investigation.

There is a difference between (1) taking what Foucault concludes
into religion and (2) thinking the question of religion with Foucault.
That difference lies in relating the analysis of power and language to
questions Foucault did not ask and doing so without being limited to
themes in his writings that explicitly hold religious content. One
problem with relying on "themes" is that it is too apt to celebrate the
fact that Foucault said something about religion without asking if his
comment truly adds to what religious thinking has already accomplished on its own. The intellectual celebrity of Foucault then tends
to overshadow the subject of religion. Carrette's comments on negative theology are particularly open to this charge since he does not
consider or compare what philosophical theology – outside of and
before Foucault – had already achieved. The Death of God movement was a particular manifestation of negative theology in the North
American setting that had indeed imagined theology in non-transcendental (or *kenosis*) forms. Foucault's analysis can add something
to negative theology, but it cannot be said to influence or inaugurate
a change in religious language from transcendence to "radical immanence." In fact, the Death of God theologians in this respect were
far more radical than Foucault. Equally, before the accomplishment
of the Death of God in the 1960s, David Friedrich Strauss had already
achieved the same breakthrough as early as the 1830s.[11] A genuine
innovation in terms of Foucault and philosophical theology does not
lie in these areas, already developed with greater sophistication than
Foucault could be expected to offer. This is no slight on Foucault; it
is just an honest admission that Foucault was not a theologian.
Though Foucault studied Christian sources, his purpose and selection were driven by curiosity about the subject, practices of *parrhesia*

11 David Friedrich Strauss is the outstanding example from the nineteenth century of a voice calling for a radical rethinking of religion. His most explicit effort to
reject theism (and the transcendental God) is *The Old Faith and the New*, a work originally published in 1872.

(mentioned above), and technologies of the self. His concern was, broadly, moral theology insofar as this identifies areas of Christian thought that can be related to the Western understanding of the self. A substantial part of this reflection is found in the unpublished fourth volume of *The History of Sexuality*. The examination of Christianity reflects Foucault's wide interest and unquestionably brilliant mind, but it is not philosophical theology. Thus, a genuine philosophical task lies beyond linking Foucault to religion and includes thinking religion with Foucault.

Yet there are examples of works that "think" religion in a Foucauldian way and that have broadly influenced my approach. One of Bernauer's earlier works, *Michel Foucault's Force of Flight*, takes the style of Foucault's thought into problems of theological ethics and provides an outstanding example of thinking with Foucault.[12] In addition, two other writers provide some context for my concern. Marc P. Lalonde has taken Foucault's analysis of power positively into liberation theology and I have benefited from his effort. This imaginative step is very much a working out of Foucault's thought in a distinctive context. Lalonde does not carry a specific theme from Foucault to his work but rather addresses a theological question in a Foucauldian manner. This is also what I hope to accomplish. In addition, the work of Thomas R. Flynn is relevant. Flynn likewise seeks to take Foucauldian thought into the questions of theology. He does not seek out areas where Foucault is suggestive of religious discourse; he rather employs Foucauldian analytical tools to raise philosophical problems and think in theological terms. Lalonde and Flynn are examples of philosophical theology in the hermeneutical spirit; they use Foucauldian thought artistically in new theological settings.

North American thought is often dominated by the social sciences, and it is worth concluding if not repeating that this work is not of that genre. I have been referred on many occasions to works, while admittedly important, that have little or nothing to do with the philosophical problems I want to encounter. I appreciate those critics who want to see a social scientific reference base, who have referred me to *The Foucault Effect* and have suggested I would be well served with reference to Ann Stoler's *Race and the Education of Desire*. I know these suggestions are meant to be helpful, and these and many other works in

---

12 Bernauer, *Michel Foucault's Force of Flight*.

the social sciences are known to me. But my particular work is in the tradition of continental philosophy, a tradition not always given a welcoming embrace in North America. In philosophical theology, there are in fact few valid references one can make to studies that take a phenomenological approach to religion and the thought of Michel Foucault. Even those authors who have most influenced my thinking and who strongly position this work – Bernauer, Flynn, and Lalonde – address what is "available"[13] to religion in Foucault but not thinking the problem of religion with Foucault. To use the word "think" in this way summons Nietzsche, Heidegger, hermeneutics, and phenomenology. These are the streams that provide the current of this work and, likewise, are the very ones in which Foucault placed his work.

13 Flynn, "Partially Desacralized Spaces," Bernauer and Carrette, *Michel Foucault and Theology*, 143–56.

1

Archaeology, Genealogy, and the Archive

MANY NORTH AMERICANS first became acquainted with Michel Foucault as a member of the new school of structuralism. Foucault actually divorced himself from this subject, but since he had made such warm remarks about it and seemed initially to accept the label as flattering, it was common to locate his thinking within this French school of thought. Its diffuse membership included the influential anthropologist Claude Lévi-Strauss, the psychoanalyst Jacques Lacan, and the ever-affable personality Roland Barthes. All these members, along with Foucault, once appeared in a French cartoon entitled "The Structuralist Picnic."[1] And given that Foucault, in the preface to *Naissance de la clinique* (1963), described his work as a "structural study,"[2] it is, to say the least, surprising that in the English translation of *The Order of Things* (1970) Foucault should confidentially advise his English-speaking readers to disregard "certain half witted commentators" in France who "persist in labelling me a 'structuralist.'" When someone like Foucault refuses to "remain the same," it is understandable that commentators are misled.[3] And while it is facile to lump Foucault and structuralism together, this environment was indeed the set of "conditions and rules" out of which Foucault spoke

1 Originally found in *La Quinzaine littéraire*, (1 July 1967), the cartoon is reproduced in Eribon, *Michel Foucault*, 176.

2 This quotation is from the English translation, *Birth of the Clinic*, xix.

3 The last recorded interview with Michel Foucault appeared in *The Advocate*. The interview was published shortly after his death and the magazine described his philosophy as a "daring system of thought known as structuralism." Though Foucault distanced himself from this discipline, on a popular level he was consistently counted among its leading representatives. *The Advocate* 400 (7 August 1984): 26–30, 58.

and of which he admittedly was "largely unaware."[4] Structuralism is a
genuine point of orientation in relation to this philosopher and to
his enterprises of archaeology and genealogy. I will not dwell on
structuralism, either here or in the chapters to follow, but it remains
the preliminary context in which to understand Foucault if not from
which to distinguish him.[5]

Structuralism for its part is often described in two forms that follow
from the foundational work of Ferdinand de Saussure's *Course in General
Linguistics.*[6] The distinctions and subtleties of structuralism, though,
rest on understanding the linguistic sign. The sign is simultaneously a
material word and a mental concept. The linguistic sign is the single
event of this signifier/signified (word/concept) relationship. British
philosophy following John Locke emphasized a similar dichotomy between the material world and ideas of the mind, but while for Locke
the connection between the world and ideas is consequential of general sensations stimulating the mind, for Saussure the origin of ideas is
not so vaguely understood. The linguistic sign is the *materiality* of ideas
that do not exist isolated in the mind but rather are integrated in general human awareness (our reasoning, our apperception, and our cultural linguistic biases). Reasoning as much as sensations are ordered in
the dynamic relationship signs hold with one another. One era of
history can have a different system of knowledge from another era due
to different arrangements and correlations of signs.

To clarify this difference, Saussure spoke of the sign's value. In effect, words hold flavour depending on their history and the context
of their appearance among other signifiers. Indeed, value has an
active sense with Saussure; the linguistic sign constantly gives rise to
value in the flux of usage, location, and relation. Saussure draws on

4 He concludes the foreword to the English edition; "It would hardly behove me,
of all people, to claim that my discourse is independent of conditions and rules of
which I am very largely unaware, and which determine other work that is being done
today." Foucault, *The Order of Things*, xiv.

5 In fact, Foucault's thought is more successfully related to the reception of phenomenology in France by way of Georges Canguilhem. See Foucault's introductory
remarks to Georges Canguilhem, *The Normal and the Pathological*, 1991.

6 Saussure, *Cours de linguistique générale.* A good case is made for the influence of
Hippolyte Taine on Saussure and some of the main arguments of linguistic structuralism. See Taine, *On Intelligence.* Also, Taine appears to be the originator of the idea of
value found in Saussure. See Aarsleff, *From Locke to Saussure*, 356–71.

the example of the French word *mouton* that in English acquires a unique culinary value. *Mouton* is an animal in French, but in English mutton is expressly an experience in dining. The two words share exactly the same Latin root but are valued differently through the dynamics of their respective linguistic families. Thus while Saussure remained sharply focused on the linguistic sign, it is easy to see how, through the idea of value, his thought suggests that linguistic signs do not have a permanent or essential meaning and that different historical eras and social settings will produce different experiences of value and meaning through the active interrelationship of signs.

In case this line of thinking seems to lead away from Foucault, we need to distinguish the two forms structuralism can take and, subsequently, the unique distinction Foucault claimed to hold. After Saussure, structuralism could assume what Hubert L. Dreyfus and Paul Rabinow distinguish as atomistic or holistic forms. On the one hand, a focus can be placed on a specific linguistic sign or set of signs and the purpose of their function. One can note how one sign or its set is distinguished from others, how it holds a sacred or profane value, how it denotes status, honour, or shame. This very "documentary" reading of the sign can be understood as atomistic. Clifford Geertz's now famous example, in *Culture and Interpretation*, of a cockfight in Bali centres almost exclusively on the single event, reading its signs in a self-referential way, and interpreting the activity independently of external political or social realities. The argument against the atomistic form of structuralism concerns its exclusively analytical vision. The question of "value" tends to rest intrinsically in the sign and, consequently, the whole analysis lacks political sophistication. Granted, in the example of Geertz's study, the cockfight as a sign performs a set of status relationships between the participants. However, Geertz does not raise the question of Bali culture, social history, or how the larger political structures of society inform the valuation of the sign in this specific event. Holistic structuralism, on the other hand, includes these larger, inclusive questions. As Dreyfus and Rabinow circumspectly comment, "what counts as an *actual* element [of value] is a function of the whole system of differences in which the element is involved."[7]

7 The "element" here is the linguistic sign. See Dreyfus and Rabinow, *Beyond Structuralism and Hermeneutics*, 53.

Foucault's project of archaeology has similarities with holistic structuralism due to its emphasis on systems of discourse and the valuation of signs in differing historical eras. At first glance, Foucault's
archaeology appears to be exactly the same as holistic structuralism
in the way he examines shifts in human reasoning from the late
Middle Ages, through the early periods of the Enlightenment, and
into the early modern era. Yet, as Foucault slowly distinguished himself from structuralism through his work in the 1960s, it becomes
apparent that his 1970 comment is apt. He never actually uses the
language typical of a structuralist study: there is no signifier/signified
dichotomy, no depth psychology, no valuation, and no synchronic
relationship of signs. In the psychoanalytic studies of Lacan the sign
plays a key role, in relation to the Id, in an effort to explain desire;
Barthes invokes the relationship of signs to describe social dichotom-
ies such as tasteful/distasteful or in (fashion)/out (of fashion) found
in contemporary culture. But Foucault is far more likely to ask the
social question. To Foucault, desire is a product of discursive activities that create the space of social reasoning in a given historical
period. In many respects, while the structuralist emphasis was on
signs and their constant movement of referring/deferring to one another, Foucault's penchant was for histories, events, and discursive
formations. Albeit, by the late 1960s it was fashionable for most
French "structuralists" to claim that they were not structuralists,
among them Foucault had possibly the best argument. Certainly with
the publication of *The Archaeology of Knowledge* Foucault indeed had
turned structuralism against itself. He began to ask how structuralism
too is an example of a linguistic formation subject to its own conditions of thought. His investigations increasingly united knowledge to
power in an attempt to understand the former as a socio-political
manifestation of the latter. To further satisfy this highly encompassing task, Foucault introduced the *episteme* (the bed of reasoning) in
which statements are found, linguistic dispersions take place, strategies are formed, linguistic economies are born, and through which
the productive activity of power circulates. But in all these expressions
it was not the "sign" he spoke of but a different term, the "statement."

Foucault distinguishes statements from linguistic signs. The distinction may seem a matter of curious semantics but it proves to be
important. The linguistic sign, certainly in the case of Lévi-Strauss
and, to a large degree, the other attendees at the Structuralist Picnic,

is a complete though elementary unit of expression. In Saussure, the sign holds together a material and conceptual side. Nevertheless, structuralism, in a subtle way, appends a third item to the event of signification. This third element is implied in the event of signing itself; it is the universal ability of humans to employ signs. To relate signs to other signs, to create or rearrange signification, requires profoundly rational acts. To Claude Lévi-Strauss the synchronic relationship of signs reveals at the same time a diachronic or deep rational structure. Lévi-Strauss used the simple illustration of a symphony score: notes appear side by side and are read from left to right, but a symphony requires a unity of musical instruments that relate down and through the sheet of music as much as to the notes that are played across it. Linguistic signs move across a surface of enunciation but they also imply a plunge downward into the universal foundations of reason. Lévi-Strauss concluded that humans have "always been thinking equally well; the improvement lies, not in an alleged progress of (the human) mind, but in the discovery of new areas to which it may apply its unchanged and unchanging powers."[8] In structuralism, the sign varies but the reasoning involved in signifying remains stable.

Foucault does not see it this way, and the "statement" is one place where his distinctive point of view is evident. As the linguistic sign implies a unified rationality, Foucault's statement implies dispersion, discontinuity, and exclusions. Foucault does not promise, as earlier commentators suggested, "order at the end"[9] and the revelation of "deep structures."[10] Rather, the task of the archaeology of knowledge is to account for the credibility of the statement or, even better, to expose how statements produce the space (location) of credible knowledge events. Foucault is fairly clear that, in the case of archaeology, he does not want to invoke the classical presuppositions of the philosophy of history: he seeks no underlying Spirit of Reason that would unify historical eras or predetermine a specific interpretation of events. "My aim was to analyze this history [of ideas], in a discontinuity that no teleology could reduce in advance; to place it [*réperer*] in a dispersion that no pre-established horizon could enclose; to

8 Lévi-Strauss, *Structural Anthropology*, 230.
9 Kurzweil, *The Age of Structuralism*, 205.
10 White, "Foucault De-coded," *History and Theory* 12, no. 1: 23.

allow it to be deployed in an anonymity on which no transcendental constitution could impose the form of the subject; to open it up to a temporality that could not promise the return of any dawn."[11]

The statement will not yield a transcendental perspective by which we can preview the movements of history; it will not unify discourses by the limits of reason; it will not offer a stable subject on which knowledge can positively rest; it will not go below the surface to touch the deep mysteries of human consciousness. In Foucault, the statement must be related to strategies. One can really deal only with a statement's effects – what it causes to be seen or stated – since it exists, so Gilles Deleuze fittingly imaged,[12] as a rhizome that is both present and hidden, local and extended. Statements locate linguistic signs, strategize them, mark the point of their emergence, but are not signs in themselves. They display for us what Foucault calls an archive: a system of "enunciability," of discursive regularities and reasonings that meet in the statement and characterize the "functioning" of an era.[13] The statement creates the credibility of what is announced. According to *The Archaeology of Knowledge*, the statement accounts for the material conditions of knowledge and defines the archive as an order of reasoning.

As Foucault travels through his analysis of the statement, he breaks it down into at least four elements. The first is the statement's modality of existence. Since the focus is not on the linguistic sign but on its performance as "sense," the statement concerns exactly how that "sign" emerges (in effect, is manufactured) in a spatio-temporal location. What relationship does the statement hold to the distribution of signs? Further, how does the statement function as a mode of distribution both for linguistic acts and for the physical and moral restrictions of an institution? Foucault is particularly concerned with the last question in *The Order of Discourse* but it is also present in *The Archaeology of Knowledge* through the idea of the statement's materiality.[14] Foucault reminds his reader that it is the "principle of dispersion and redistribution," not that of formulation, that he is after; the important thing, therefore, is to ask how linguistic acts function as

11 Foucault, *L'archéologie du savoir*, 264–5.
12 Deleuze and Guattari, *A Thousand Plateaus*.
13 Foucault, *The Archaeology of Knowledge*, 129.
14 Ibid., 100–3.

credible events in the various institutional contexts, be they clinical, psychiatric, or economic, that Foucault ably identifies as the archives of history.[15]

The second element, certainly of equal importance, is precisely that Foucault is talking about history in a particular way. While he shuns the notion of the "history of ideas," which to him amounts to a forced reading, his statement remains an element of historical investigation. "The history of ideas," as Foucault would have us think of the phrase, sees philosophy as an evolutionary procession. Ideas supersede one another by the steady refinement of culture until at last a crescendo is reached. In such an approach, the author of the great idea must be identified as well as the refinements of the great student. But, with the statement, Foucault wants to exhibit knowledge anonymously, relating it not to individuals but to systems of production – to archival permission, as I will explain – that create epistemological sites and open temporal events in an archive. Knowledge in Foucault does not advance but rather happens or disperses itself only to be subject again to disruption, exclusion, recombination, and re-formation. This is why an archive of history, distinct from an epoch or era, is a most suitable term. Discovering the institutional distribution of discursive events by the presence of the statement is akin to opening a display of knowledge. This historical analysis does not "question things said" but questions them "as to their mode of existence." The quest is not for truth (that is, an objective content) but for the operation of truth as an archive event.

The third element of significance is the way in which the statement is ironically invisible when it is present. Foucault speaks of the "quasi-invisibility of the 'there is,' [*il y a*]." He makes his point clearer when he subsequently describes the limited existence of a linguistic event. The statement only makes present the moment, the "flash of meaning" [*éclair du sens*] of the event of the sign.[16] The statement does not, however, lie behind the sign as its true meaning. It simply structures it. Like the sign itself, the statement is "there" in relation to other

15 In conversation with students in Los Angeles in 1976, Foucault stated, "What interests me in the problem of discourse is the fact that somebody has said something at one moment. I do not wish to stress the meaning, but the function of the fact that this thing has been spoken by somebody at this point. That is what I call the event." Foucault, "Dialogue on Power" (Centre Michel Foucault, Document 533).

16 Foucault, *L'archéologie du savoir*, 147; *The Archaeology of Knowledge*, 112.

statements that compose the archive and position the presentation of the sign. But one cannot infer that in some manner "presence" is rooted in deep meaning or related back to the profound origins of human language. The statement function is simply *being present for the sign* (being the "there is") as the order of its appearance. Almost simultaneously, *being present* is equally being absent, for the statement disperses signs by the act of making present the sign's referential potential. The sign *signs* another sign – language circles in perpetual self-reference – with the statement merely coordinating the "sense" of the signing event. The statement makes the event present, brings it to the fore, but the statement is immediately absent in the very definition of this activity. Presence is the moment and therefore can never be more than the "already there"; its permanent effect is that of having already been. The statement in this way is a sign of nothing; it accounts only for the position of signs but must be the "already been" in the act of the sign. This permanent play of presenting yet being absent eliminates the possibility of understanding the statement as a thing. It is not a thing but a strategy of things. It brings us into the present of an archive exactly by displaying knowledge equally as an experience of the archive. The statement in this sense is strangely more experiential than it is analytical.

A fourth element: the statement understood as a form. Here one can highlight a facet of *The Archaeology of Knowledge* that implies and calls forward the later adaptations of genealogy (specifically refined in *The Order of Discourse* but far more dramatically elaborated in *Discipline and Punish*). At this point, one must begin to see that in all practical ways archaeology and what Foucault later develops as genealogy assist the same investigation. In the Western tradition the notion of a form habitually recalls Plato and the grand metaphysical narratives of philosophy like truth, justice, and love. In terms of the statement, this *idealistic* (ειδοσ) residue of platonic inclination must be resisted. In the archive the form relates to strategies rather than to preconceptual patterns of thought or pre-given ends to thought. An archive form is not the universal idea, let us say, of "tree-ness" necessarily pre-given to the physical apprehension of trees in all their variety. In the archive, the abstract does not precede the concrete. Rather, the reasoning of things is an event of strategies carved out by statements and occupied by signs. The statement, therefore, actively formulates – circulates as it produces – the perception of the real. It is a form of the economy of meaning. Hence, one must note that the statement, though Foucault speaks of its simultaneous presence and absence, is not a passive and silent partner of events. The involvement of the statement and its economy in the actual moment makes it a "form" of archival perception in a very particular way. To be grasped, this understanding must involve more than the linguistic sign. Foucault considers the precedent weight of historical forces, the circulation of power in the archive, the physical architecture of buildings, the office of the speaker in relation to the audience, the place of a proposition within a specific discipline, the social reputation of certain expressions, etc. All these competing factors will define the new study of genealogy. They are the material elements of the statement, all meticulously reviewed in works following *The Archaeology of Knowledge* but nevertheless effectively constituted in that work as the functioning "field of use" in which a statement is found.[17] The materiality of the statement, Foucault holds, creates a "repeatable" experience. A form, then, is not limited to the activity of statements carving out space but includes the repetition of the statement on an institutional level. A "form" creates a repeatable experience – a replication of order and meaning. Foucault states in summary, "The system [*régime*] of materiality that statements necessarily obey is therefore the order of the institution rather than the spatio-temporal localization; it defines *possibilities of reinscription and transcription* (but also thresholds and limits), rather than limited and perishable individualities."[18] The statement as form is a way of describing the capacity of the statement to hold an archive experience in place, however momentarily, as a field of regularity, as a system of limitation, and as an experience of repetition. When a form begins to crumble by shifts in the foundation or through the transgression of expectations, so too does the statement, and its economy evaporates from the scene or washes away "like a face drawn in the sand at the edge of the sea."[19]

Yet, has Foucault satisfactorily answered how statements can shift in meaning, collapse, and recombine? Has he given enough evidence to support the claim that knowledge is a product uniquely related to archival strategies? And what about the materiality of the statement,

17   Foucault, *L'archéologie du savoir, 137* (translation mine).
18   Ibid., 136 (translation mine).
19   Foucault, *The Order of Things*, 387.

its institutional standing, its being seen and being heard as well as its being spoken? Arguably none of these questions are addressed until genealogy and power enter the conversation.

FOUCAULT AND GENEALOGY

In an interview Foucault stated that he had escaped phenomenology by way of Friedrich Nietzsche.[20] What could he have meant by "escape"? Of course, the comment implies that phenomenology is a trap, but what then is the trap?

Foucault claimed that the primary question in his earliest writing was whether transcendental phenomenology could adequately account for the experience of the subject.[21] Phenomenology, we need to recall, rests its hermeneutical considerations on a stable subject, thereby opening to discussion the interrelation of ego and judgment or pure consciousness and pure experience. Structuralism, though much less elaborate, equally rested its basic act of signification on a universal constant buried in the subject. True, structuralism made no appeal to pure consciousness, but it did rely on transcendental reason. The trap Foucault spoke of may consist of the inability of these transcendental models to liberate hermeneutical questions from a self-referential system. The knowledge a subject holds must be ironically grounded upon a universal element found in the subject. Thus, the presupposition of subjectivity gives authority to systems of discourse that hold onto, in the words of Husserl, the utopian dream of one day arriving at "the total field of possible research" called "the World."[22] But that presupposition, due to its circular structure, continually recedes deeper and deeper into a secret origin.

Strictly speaking, it was not Nietzsche who convinced Foucault to renounce the idea that "beyond any apparent beginning there is always a secret origin,"[23] whether that origin is phenomenology's pure consciousness or structuralism's deeply reasoning subject. But Nietzsche clearly undermined both disciplines when he examined the question of reason in history. Nietzsche saw no original stability

20 Foucault, "Structuralism and Post-Structuralism: An Interview with Michel Foucault" (Centre Michel Foucault, Document 105). This interview was conducted by Gérard Raulet, translated by Jeremy Harding, and published in *Telos*.

21 Foucault, "Structuralism and Post-Structuralism," 199.

22 Husserl, *Ideas: General Introduction to Pure Phenomenology*.

23 Foucault, *The Archaeology of Knowledge*, 25; *L'archéologie du savoir*, 36.

or point of departure but rather talked of arbitrary formations related to domination, descent, and disparity.[24] From Nietzsche Foucault picked up on the subterfuge of power involved in linguistic formations and archival experiences. Perhaps this was not so much an escape from a "trap"– no doubt a bit of hyperbole on the part of Foucault – but certainly it was a change in perspective. When power is mixed in with linguistic formations, the question moves from the utopian foundation of knowledge and its correspondence to reality to knowledge recognized inexorably as a political now. Far more convincingly than archaeology alone, genealogy introduces an understanding of knowledge not only as an event emerging from linguistic forms and material locations but also as a product of their recombinant activity. In other words, genealogy is about the anonymity of knowledge as an effect of power – its expression, its space, its present. It is as if to say that power is knowledge by another name.

In his book *Foucault's Nietzschean Genealogy*, Michael Mahon correctly identifies Foucault's "Nietzsche, Genealogy, and History"[25] as a "landmark essay that signals the explicit adoption of Nietzschean approaches."[26] Though Foucault seemed to feel that his two concerns with language and power always complemented each other,[27] Mahon shows how power becomes an explicit axis of investigation that at times displaces the archaeological fixation on the statement. "Archaeology proceeds along the truth axis, analyzing discursive conditions of existence. Genealogy travels the power axis, examining culturally true discourse's insertion into institutional and other non-discursive practices."[28] Only on the power axis is language accordingly a mode of subjugation, that is, a mode of the production of experience. Language combined with power is how one speaks of the genealogy of knowledge in an archive.

Foucault defines genealogy with two broad strokes taken from Nietzsche. One is the notion of descent, and the second is that of emergence. Foucault translated Nietzsche's *Herkunft* ("origin" in terms of one's background or extraction) as descent (*la souche* and *la provenance*).[29] But he means in particular the markings or weight of

24 Foucault, "Nietzsche, la généalogie, l'histoire," *Dites et écrits*, 136–56.
25 Foucault, *Language, Counter-Memory, Practice*, 139–64.
26 Mahon, *Foucault's Nietzschean Genealogy*, 105–6.
27 Foucault, "Nietzsche, la généalogie, l'histoire," 150.
28 Mahon, *Foucault's Nietzschean Genealogy*, 105
29 Foucault, *Dites et écrits*, 140.

history on the body or found in the interpretation of an event. That is, descent describes forms of domination, both discursive and non-discursive, in which power is both *force* and *location*. Events are "disparate" insofar as by descending Foucault means they scatter and recombine. And while this happens in an arbitrary way, it is by no means innocent. The circulation of power plays actively on linguistic forms: it produces an interpretive location or space in the archive. Language is not equal among those who employ it. The social status of the speaker, or the office a speaker holds, is a location in an archive that weighs on the formation of "truth." Specific types of authority interrupt the flow of power, redirect it, and predispose it. In the archive, power constricts one form of expression and permits others. Its form of control is by means of limitations and openings. In this sense, power is that which opens the archive or forms spaces of display. Foucault accordingly sees the activity of power wholly positively. Power is not a depressing force; it is not "oppression," though it can certainly be used to oppress. Power is the force of openings and closures, of horizons and restrictions, that permits the manifestation of discourse.

Entstehung, likewise from Nietzsche, is another elaboration of genealogy found in Foucault. The German word means "arising" and can imply "formation." Foucault translated this word as "emergence" (*émergence*), which is completely acceptable, but through this translation moves beyond Nietzsche's intentions. To Foucault emergence expresses the active relationship of forces that accounts for the fluctuation of power and the competition of events in an archive. In such activity, forces multiply locations for discursive and non-discursive practices. The images here are very spatial. For example, Foucault can speak of heterotopias or other spaces where certain forms of life or reasoning reside apart from more dominant yet contemporary forms. Thus, specific social practices may hold "centre stage" at one point in history only to be invaded from the outside and disrupted or reformulated.[30] The reality of power, in Foucault, is the constant competition of forces that accounts for the general sense of instability in an archive. This is not to say that an archive is permanently unstable, but more accurately that the transformation of an archive is not related to the hidden progress of reason. Transformations are the consequence of fluctuations in the competition of forces. They are anonymous, plural, and

30 Foucault, "Nietzsche, la généalogie, l'histoire," 150.

simultaneous practices of particular forms. In Foucault, it is most certainly practices that create openings for specific events of knowledge rather than reason being the foundation for the practice knowledge.

Foucault uses *emergence* to display the competition of forces: "the isolation of different points of emergence does not conform to the successive configurations of an identical meaning; rather, they result from substitutions, displacements, disguised conquests, and systematic reversals."[31] I want to use the word "permission" as a way to understand emergence as an effect of power. By permission I mean to identify how credible space is opened epistemologically to an agent by means of the competitive relationships of force. Permission identifies the weight of precedent historical events, the manner in which such events anticipate areas immediately on the horizon and, as such, attract new epistemological formulations or permit these formulations a credible reception. The Panopticon of *Discipline and Punish* is a most obvious platform on which to portray this function, but Foucault gives many others. In *Madness and Civilization* Foucault describes a shift from the society of exclusion to the society of incarceration. Permission indicates how the former society opens on an epistemological level a space that anticipates or receives the latter order. The space of incarceration invades from the outside those practices already established in exclusion; thus, practices of exclusion *permitted* spaces of reversal and reformulation that defined incarceration.

In volume 2 of the *History of Sexuality* Foucault claims that archaeology had allowed him to examine the forms of truth whereas genealogy allowed him to examine practices out of which these forms emerged.[32] The two movements of archaeology and genealogy, then, are to be united in the examination of an archive. The first involves the examination of the statement through which linguistic practices are formed, and the second involves the examination of power through which such formations actively produce the space of credible events. The archive is both the field on which these dynamics are displayed and the descent of their competition. These two basic movements in Foucault invite an encounter with the production of meaning as an event and as a problem for theology.

31 Ibid., 151.
32 Foucault, *The Uses of Pleasure*, 11–12.

2

Statements and Space in the Archive

FOUCAULT'S DEFINITION OF THE STATEMENT is often circuitous and unsatisfactory. Instead of a succinct description, he delivers a set of warnings. "A statement does not have a correlate confronting it (as if in a face to face relation) ... as a proposition has a referent (or lacks one) or as a proper noun designates someone (or no one)."[1] The statement does not have an author who is "the cause, origin, or point of departure for the phenomenon of the written or spoken sentence."[2] And further, it is "not sufficient to state a sentence" or "to state it in relation to a particular field of objects or in relation to a particular subject."[3] These words of warning serve as a guide but regretfully not as an answer to the question, What is the statement?

We already know, and the comments above serve to reinforce, that the first act when considering the statement is to forget about structuralism. The statement is not a string of signs that may be examined individually; rather, it involves the more complete notion of the formation of knowledge. But even at this level, we do not necessarily mean that the statement is generally a description reflecting an observation. Indeed, a statement is not necessarily a vocalization. A statement can be a setting of architecture or, at the very least, how material things are arranged – the view from where I am standing, the building that inhibits or permits sight lines – as much as it can be the language employed in the claim that "I am here."[4] Understanding

1 Mahon, *Foucault's Nietzschean Genealogy*, 120
2 Ibid., 125.
3 Ibid., 128.
4 Foucault, *The Archaeology of Knowledge*, 51-2. This elaboration on my part is influenced by Deleuze and it relates to what Foucault called the "institutional site."

the statement includes understanding it as an event.[5] It is an event in the archaeology of knowledge. It is an occupation within a formation of space. It is the "this now" of the archive field; it is even the why of "this now" as an order of experience. The statement is the relationship, the meeting place, of both the articulated and non-articulated; the crossing of paths and positioning of acts; the *episteme* of the present, the reason of reasoning, that creates in this place this archive as a way of being (ordering) in the world.

With Foucault, the definition of a statement attracts many descriptions simultaneously: unhappily, none are intended to be final or authoritative. The tentativeness of the act of defining goes hand in hand with the insight that the statement is the condition of things rather than the correlation of words to things. Things "emerge" and statements mark locations of emergence. Things stand in history, and statements mark the platform of standing if not the contours of being-there. Archives are always a question of strategies, of the arrangement of things that "make sense"[6] or hold together as order. The order of sense in one archive or another is the result of a strategy;[7] thus, with the statement, Foucault seeks to define a regime. The archive is a regime of truth, a productivity of statements that witness in their fact the form of the archive they occupy. So, while the statement may be composed of signs, it is not a sign. While it includes words, it is not a phrase or sentence. While it can be displayed in architectural arrangements, it is not architecture. A statement is, rather, the condition in which a sign, physical or linguistic, functions and that enables a regime of knowledge to exist.

The statement, because it variously forms the order of things from one archive to another, is no abstract bystander. The statement, though complex in definition, does not suggest a metaphysical reality. What is stated is "located" in the sense that it has identity (situation) within a strategy of truth, within a politics of language. The actually stated is not, then, necessarily the "statement." Rather, the statement is necessary to the comprehensibility of the "event" it is identifying in the act of articulation or, more generally, in the

5 Foucault, *The Archaeology of Knowledge*, 41, 127–31. The notion of the "event" in this work derives from Foucault's description of "the system that governs the appearance of statements as unique events" (129).

6 Foucault, *The Archaeology of Knowledge*, 86.

7 Ibid., 80

functioning of institutions. Statements are events because they are discursive groupings (words) and non-discursive relations (things) that emerge to express epistemic strategies.

Since the statement highlights a point of emergence in a strategic field, its definition must encompass the archive as the exterior setting that enables its possibility. The statement must be imagined fundamentally outside the subject who is, nevertheless, the material witness to its expression. If the archive can be imagined as a set of intersecting lines that forge the berth of a style of reasoning (the *episteme*), the statement is a point of intersection or *rencontre* that activates that style specifically. Here in particular Foucault counteracts the transcendental search for a subjective identity by claiming that the author, as much as the subject (both of whom in traditional phenomenological philosophy stand in the background as the "authority"), is not the origin but the function of the statement. The author does not originate discourse so much as coordinate it or at best initiate a certain style; and the meaning of that coordination, which is specific to the *episteme* in which it has emerged, remains unknown finally even to the individual author.

Sigmund Freud, Foucault maintained, is not an author but an *epistemic* event. That is, Freud initiated a discursive style or practice, but that practice is really a composite of statements; it is even a "new" statement that governs an entire set of related and competing discursive events. Freud could never know the whole of that new strategy of discourse, or necessarily grasp all its variant expressions, even though he initiated it. Freud, who is an author-function, must be distinguished from the writer who was (as much as his disciples) subject to the rules of the discursive formation that enabled his analysis. At the level of the statement, his author-function was anonymous to his self-identity as the practising psychoanalyst.[8]

To be sure, this does not mean that the statement prevents a theory from being traced to its inventor or an expression from being attributed to the one who coined it. But these particular identifications necessarily assume an already active field of statements that empowers them. That field is a productive environment from which no single point of origin can be isolated. In the archive, every point is understood within the complex of its local community, and no point

8 See Foucault, "What Is an Author?" Adams and Searle, *Critical Theory since 1965*, 138–48.

can make sense without implying the function of the local community. In the archive, the supreme question is location and the supreme deception is originality.

Despite several abstract and obscure ways of approaching the statement, Foucault arrives at some cogent definitions. Foucault shifts the reader's focus from linguistic acts to the formation of reasoning in the space of the archive. He opens dimensions in the archive and challenges us with images of differing and competing experiences of space and language. In short, a statement is a "discursive formation" that holds a certain style or weight defined by the manner in which it occupies archival space. Of all the commentators on Foucault, Gilles Deleuze grasped this essential idea most radically.

Deleuze speaks of three orders of space that relate the statement to the field of its appearance. He calls them collateral space, correlative space, and complementary space. He emphasizes the dynamic or active manner in which an archive is not only an occupation of space but equally its transformation. Archives compose unique settings that limit the event of a statement to particular meanings or sets of meaning. The statement therefore cannot be indefinite; rather it is a constricted event within the *episteme* of its appearance and within which it stands. Accordingly, the strategy of the archive holds the statement in endurance; that is, strategy makes the statement "present" as the endurance of the archive. Henri Bergson, Deleuze believes, describes the same phenomenon with his notion of memory,[9] where an element continues to exist as long as the space that structures it continues to preserve it.[10] Consequently, the activity of the archive is the activity of sustaining statements, and this means finally that statements are spaces of *epistemic* proportion.

Deleuze uses collateral space to refer to the manner in which statements can wander across fields of reference and, in this act, transform one location by the reasoning of another. He tells us that a statement "operates neither laterally nor vertically but transversally."[11] This means that in its manifest location a statement can refer to any contemporaneous region in the archive: the statement can express the "order of the archive" in such a way that the

9 Bergson, *Matter and Memory*, 204–23.
10 Deleuze, *Foucault*, 5.
11 Ibid.

original event is redeployed heterogeneously in different archival functions and different locations. Statements, then, include a concern about the overlapping structures of space. They are not about lines that connect locations but about orders that invade locations and sometimes re-order the sense of a location. Further, the strategy of space in one location can be enacted simultaneously (collaterally) in multiple locations. "Even when they seem to operate in the same language, statements of a discursive formation move from description to observation, calculation, institution and prescription, and use several systems or languages in the process."[12] Collateral space describes the varied relationships in which a statement is engaged by the sheer fact of the diverse locations that claim its meaning. Indeed, the statement brings spaces into competition. Foucault demonstrated this by showing how the same set of statements can be associated with elementary schools and military colleges; in this instance, statements that emerge in one setting of the disciplinary archive can fluctuate and re-locate or re-signify the reasoning of another setting. Thus, collateral space is a description of the anonymity of statement dispersion across the spaces of the archive.

   Some significant points about collateral space, however, seem to elude Deleuze and perhaps even stretch the thought of Foucault. First, the archive as a setting plays the role of limiting the statement-event despite its movement collaterally. The statement as a strategy remains restricted to the potential the archive offers it. The statement remains, at the very least, within the horizon of the archive that manifests it. Granted, a statement may indeed be at the very limit of that horizon; it may even seek to defy the *episteme* in which it appears, but the statement cannot be impossible to the order that manifests its presence. Deleuze simply claims that statements cannot be *just anything*; rather, they are to be associated "with the rules governing the particular field in which they are distributed and reproduced."[13] The whole field of the distribution and reproduction of statements and the composite collateral spaces involved in this activity is the archive field of permission. Though Foucault affirms that statements can appear "outside" a given order, the "outside" must still remain in the horizon of the archive in question – it is still a possibility within the

12 Ibid.
13 Ibid., 4.

permission of the horizon. So, for example, a classical statement from the seventeenth century related to the king's body can have a form of being in the disciplinary space of nineteenth-century constitutional government.[14] But the statement of the body is now reformulated as a permissible order of knowledge in the new archive. It is not the "outside" of the archive so much as it is the apprehension of an outside within the permission of the given archive. This observation will be key when considering how one archive order can invade another, but here, at the level of collateral space, the crucial point is that the shifting of statements within the spaces of an archive are to be understood as part of the limitations of *permission* the archive gives to the statement.

A second element that seems to be missing in Deleuze's analysis of collateral space is the critical question of the a priori status of the statement. By his silence, Deleuze implies that whether archive space or statements come first is at best immaterial and certainly irrelevant. It can be argued, on the contrary, that while the answer is elusive (for statements produce space, but space is needed for the production of statements), the question is not useless. Posing the question actually serves to orient how, at another level, the relationship between archaeology and genealogy will be understood; it is also central, as a question, to imagining how one archive can fall apart and be displaced by another. If archaeology is about the order (*episteme*) of statements and genealogy is about the transformation of archives, then it is important to ask whether the formation of statements involves equally the transformation of space. Is the activity of the statement in effect the production of space?

Deleuze might well want to avoid an enquiry that potentially invokes an a priori element such as the statement – a Kantian category, as it were. The a priori question suggests a return to a philosophy of metaphysics, which would almost render absurd the effort thus far to define history as both an arbitrary and an anonymous series of strategies, locations, and events. But the question haunts Deleuze as he takes his reader through the subtleties of Foucault. Meanwhile, it seems, even Foucault knows that the question lurks in the background, but contrary to Deleuze, he faces the question head-on. Foucault takes direct aim at the status of the a priori in what is

14 Foucault, "Truth and Power," *Power/Knowledge*, 109–33.

arguably the central chapter of *The Archaeology of Knowledge*. In fact, Foucault claims, archaeology brings us face to face with the question and the meaning of the a priori in philosophy. Archaeology transforms the question such that the archivist is no longer dealing with formal (transcendental) ideals: at the level of archaeology, the a priori "does not constitute, above events, and in an unmoving heaven, an atemporal structure."[15] Foucault's a priori is the archive itself; it is the "historical a priori" that is "the law of what can be said, the system that governs the appearance of statements as unique events."[16] It seems that the archive – a strategy of space – is given before the comprehensibility of the statement; the archive is the "law" of that comprehensibility. Yet, curiously, having made these claims, Foucault is rather reluctant to accept them himself. The problem is that as the given statement-event forms the archive, the permission of the archive is necessarily already active. The archive is the "present" of the statement even though the statement-event composes the archive and can transform it. There is a built-in tautology, but it is exactly this that creates the difference between Foucault and Kant. In Foucault, spaces are multiple and simultaneous. The sense of space as an a priori does not rest on stability but on variability. We cannot descend a ladder of formal logic that starts at the top and deductively moves downward. The archive is not an ideal of transcendence that is to be recovered within the experience of imminence. Rather, the archive is the constant engagement of spaces permitting the manifestation of statement-events and statement-events creating spaces in their manifestation. Spaces and the statement compose dynamically the moment in the archive as the "event." Consequently, in the archive the question of the a priori remains a practical one geared to addressing history at the level of variation and disruption.

This is why, or at least substantially why, Foucault describes the statement not as a mark of stability but of instability. Its very presence in collateral space, as defined by Deleuze, means that the statement is disturbing, that it is a centre of dispersion, that its effect on its location includes the potential of producing new strategies that would alter the very space of the event or reverse its sense. Foucault claims that in fact in the archive a historical a priori exists in the dynamics

15 Foucault, *The Archaeology of Knowledge*, 127.
16 Ibid., 129.

of statements as strategies of space. Indeed the dynamics here exposed define the basic insight of genealogy. Statements occupy space but equally produce it. Statements mark momentary points of stability but are themselves and simultaneously the power of instability. Archaeology addresses the limits of the statement, its form (event), and its formation (strategy). But when Deleuze dismisses the question of the a priori he unknowingly also dismisses the insight that at the heart of his "collateral spaces" lies the instability that introduces later genealogical investigations. "The reason for using this rather barbarous term [a priori]," Foucault tells us, "is that this a priori must take account of the statements in their dispersion, in all the flaws opened up by their non-coherence, in their overlapping and mutual replacement, in the simultaneity, which is not unifiable, and in their succession, which has not only a meaning or a truth, but a history, and a specific history that does not refer it back to the laws of an alien development [i.e., not back to a transcendental or formal a priori]."[17] The collateral spaces of archaeology, then, are not clearly comprehended unless the unstable nature of the kind of a priori that concerns Foucault is accommodated to express the alterations of historical experience.

Deleuze's analysis remains impressive nevertheless, and he is one of the few commentators to examine, at a high level of sophistication, the question of the statement and the spaces of the archive. Though Deleuze, I feel, inappropriately divorces genealogy from archaeology – something most commentators see as misleading – when he moves to his second and third descriptions of archaeological space, he proves very able. Deleuze takes Foucault beyond Foucault, using greater philosophical acumen, yet he does not take the reader, inappropriately, away from Foucault or from insight inspired by Foucault.

With correlative space, the second avenue of investigation for Deleuze, we encounter the restriction on space imposed by the practice of the statement. The statement-event can produce multiple forms of space occupation or strategies, but it must necessarily occupy space and perform strategies. Thus, in the act of its performance, the statement defines the horizon of its experience. For example, the act of writing a letter is not an isolated act of recording information for the addressee. It is also a practice that, in its activity,

17 Ibid., 127.

opens up a function of space. The statement-practice, which in this case is the act of letter-writing, positions the writer within the broader functions of the archive. The practice "pre-forms" the impression (interpretation) of the event. When I encounter the letter writer, the activity of the writer influences the interpretive horizon of the space I am entering. In this sense, the statement is a performance of space as much as it is an event in the language of space. A letter implies a writer, and a contract, Deleuze states, an underwriter. The occupation of space in these acts constantly disposes the horizon of the statement-event to a specific context or interpretation. The effect here recalls the phenomenological descriptions of Hans-Georg Gadamer and the "fore-perception" of an event.[18] Neither Foucault nor Deleuze refers to phenomenology in this case, but they could have with good results. In place of such assistance we must imagine with little help how the event of the statement holds a correlative relationship to the practical space it occupies. We must imagine that when the statement emerges it is "already there" as a form of occupation. It has already been read, seen, articulated because its enactment is necessarily already in correlation to a function. The act of letter-writing, to continue the example, is already the "space of the letter" before the letter is written. The notion of the "already" is significant and will need to be carried forward in our investigation. For the moment this can be understood as the functional aspect of the statement (correlative) as opposed to the variable aspect of the statement (collateral).

Deleuze concludes his characterizations of correlative space by returning to the notion of anonymity. As Foucault spoke of an author-function, correlative space refers in a general way to the anonymity of archival functions. Archives force us beyond the question of identity, beyond the habit of relating specific acts to personal deliberations. Archive spaces operate beyond consciousness and control. "Foucault echoes Blanchot," Deleuze reports, "in denouncing all linguistic personology and seeing the different positions for the speaking subject as located within a deep anonymous murmur."[19] Subjective identities are shattered in Foucault. Identity is at best an effect if not an illusion of archive functions – of statements that form. The subject is merely,

18 See Hans-Georg Gadamer, *Truth and Method*, 265-71; Gadamer's discussion is rooted in Martin Heidegger, *Being and Time*.
19 Deleuze, *Foucault*, 7.

perhaps even accidentally, the impression of linguistic systems that imply if not create the location of agency. Thus, as Foucault opened his inaugural lecture at the Collège de France, he both celebrated and mourned the lack of correlative space that offered the anonymity he valued: "rather than taking up words myself, I prefer to be enveloped by them and taken well beyond all possible beginnings."[20] Here he speaks of employing a function – an office that can carry his explorations anonymously – rather than being a function (a professor or a newly crowned *savant*) through the illusion of personal identity.

Deleuze calls the third order complementary space. Foucault spoke of a *rapprochement*[21] between discursive formations and non-discursive domains. This is perhaps a play with language that hints of exaggeration, and one might find Deleuze's description of complementary space as a liaison between the statement and its "institutional milieu" more helpful."[22] But it must be remembered that complementary space does not involve a direct connection between a language and an institution. Foucault never reduces language to the functions and activities of an institutional setting. He never allows the conclusion that classical medical discourse, for example, led inexorably to certain practices of confinement. With collateral space one speaks of statement-events being present in different practical settings, and with correlative space one speaks of functions pre-forming and constricting the statement-event horizon. With complementary space Deleuze moves in a third direction. Between institutions (material statements) and statement-events there lies a diagonal relationship. Deleuze does not mean that statement-events defer to institutional practices (horizontally as in poststructuralism), nor does he mean that the statement-event rests on an institutional practice (vertically as in structuralism). "Between the non-discursive formations of institutions and the discursive formations of statements, there is a great temptation to establish either a sort of vertical parallelism ... or a horizontal causality ... "[23] In place of these two options, the diagonal relationship between statements and institutions defines a tensive apposition between them. The non-discursive (or material) statement

20 Foucault, *L'Ordre du discours*, 7 (translation mine).
21 Foucault, *Archéologie du savoir*, 212.
22 Deleuze, *Foucault*, 9.
23 Ibid.

and the discursive statement-event both produce and limit each other. Institutions carve out archival fields; discursive activities create interpretive potentials in relation to the field in question. There is no direct correlation between them, but there is certainly a relationship of competition. Institutional settings are the occasion of statement strategies and, often, the prerequisite of the social authority the strategy holds. The political office already gives texture (such as gravity and authority) to the language employed by it; similarly, the statement-event (the strategic arrangement of language in this case) becomes the associative horizon of the office. Between the institutional texture and the associated horizon lie the linkages of complementary space. Deleuze speaks of this as a diagonal relationship precisely because, in place of a direct correlation, he seeks influences, mutual limitations, and consequent revisions.[24] Inasmuch as a political office, for example, is the material statement of an event, it equally is the site of potential invasions of differently ordered statement-events. The politician can suddenly be the martyr or the scapegoat. The older structuralist sense of the sign and the signified is too simplistic to accommodate such mutations, reverses, and ruptures in the fabric of the archive. However, it is precisely part of archaeological analysis to account for them. Once again, we touch the coattails of a soon to be developed genealogy, but immediately it is evident that ruptures in the archive exist because direct correlations do not exist. Diagonal competition rather than direct relation defines the archive in terms of archaeology, the statement, and its spaces.

One might rightly ask Deleuze why then use the word "complementary" for this portrayal of competitive space? Deleuze, at this point, is simply offering an image on which to build a more explicit description of power and genealogy. He states unequivocally, "Foucault's readers become aware of the fact that we are entering into a new domain, that of power and its relation to knowledge, which is to be explained in the sequel to *Archaeology*."[25] At this point Deleuze sees his task as limited to identifying the two types of statements that complement each other while occupying the same location: the material statement (which on one occasion Foucault called the "statement-

24 Ibid., 10.
25 Ibid., 12.

thing"[26]) and the statement-event. Complementary space describes the forms of these two statements. One form is the seeing of the statement: the material statement of architecture or the authority of an office. The other form is the articulation of the statement. The latter involves a regime of knowledge that the statement-event invokes. Complementary space is used to identity these two aspects of the statement unfolding in one location. The Panopticon, for example, has pronounced lines of vision, employees who hold an office, and diverse locations for the statement-event in relation to guards and prisoners. Presently, however, complementary space recognizes generally how two elements of the statement can be simultaneous, in competition, and definitive of the setting of the archive. In all these aspects, complementary space leads inescapably to the analyses of genealogy.

Two points might be made in review before proceeding. First, while it is difficult to define statements, and while one might even say that Foucault himself is no help, it is clear that a statement is not the same as a phrase, sentence, or proposition. To be sure, the statement-event involves language, but in effect it identifies a location within the order of archival space. For its part, the work of archaeology is exactly the investigation of that order. Second, it is fairly clear that behind the scene of Foucault's archaeology lies the genealogical question of power. To a degree, Foucault misses this in the *Archaeology of Knowledge* by paying too much attention to his division between the material statement (or statement-thing) and the statement-event. Yet, all the language of genealogy is there: "horizons," "shifts," "formations," "transformations," and "discontinuities." In his archaeological analysis, Foucault had not yet found a way to portray the activity of statements in relation to the formation of strategies, and he accomplishes precisely this with the turn to power.

26 Foucault, *The Archaeology of Knowledge*, 129.

3

Genealogy and Archive Spaces

ACCORDING TO FOUCAULT, the reintroduction of Roman law into Western discourse in the twelfth century is a pivotal moment in Western history. He considered it, in fact, the foundation of the modern *episteme*.

> This resurrection of Roman law had in effect a technical and constitutive role to play in the establishment of the authoritarian, administrative, and, in the final analysis, absolute power of the monarchy. And when this legal edifice escapes in later centuries from the control of the monarch, when, more accurately, it is turned against that control, it is always the limits of this sovereign power that are put in question, its prerogatives that are challenged. In other words, I believe that the King remains the central personage in the whole legal edifice of the West.[1]

Using the techniques of archaeology, we can say that Roman law is the material statement (or statement-thing) that opens spaces of permission in the Western social matrix. In this sense, in the archive, the material statements are the horizon in which the cluster of statement-events gathers as the form of (even, are the forms of) power. In the case of monarchical power, which is Foucault's primary example, power, because it is elusive and constitutive, formative and dynamic, eventually accounts for the reversed and altered locations of the statement-event. Monarchical power returns as juridical power. The move from the former archive to the latter cannot be reduced to a

1 Foucault, *Power/Knowledge*, 94.

single factor but must rather incorporate the archive horizon – the permission that lies at the fringe and in the fluctuations of power.

The ebb and flow is clear: power escapes the limits of one formulation only to return with new vigour. Power reformulates the archive because it turns back, as it were, from the horizon; the vengeance of power is the epistemic shift of the archive. Here, then, is no explanation of archive development through progressive stages but rather a display of the shifting guises of power that re-create "sense" (*episteme*) through sheer anonymous mutation. This basic constructing and deconstructing character of power is uniquely integrated with the concept of the archive in Foucault as genealogy.

Discipline and Punish is the most significant of Foucault's genealogical investigations. Through the notion of sovereignty and its reversal, Foucault melds power with archaeology while upholding the archive as the frame or setting of epistemic forms. Using Kantorowitz as a guide,[2] Foucault presents the social experience of the Middle Ages as made up of the king's two bodies. The king in the Middle Ages has of course an individual body but is equally the body politic. Sovereignty is the unique property of the monarch and unavailable to the subjects. As the king lives, so goes the state: the pleasure of the king is the pleasure of the state, and if the king is insulted, so too are the subjects of the nation. In the Middle Ages, the administrative functions of the royal court extended the body of the king to the most common orders of daily life.

Foucault catalogues the formation of the modern disciplinary society as the reverse of monarchical sovereignty to demonstrate the critical value of genealogy. Horrific scenes drawn from the account of Robert-François Damiens' execution open *Discipline and Punish* and set the stage for Foucault's masterful presentation. All the orders of space that Deleuze defined with great philosophical flare are present and play out in and through the suffering of a condemned body. Damiens is the condemned. His helplessness includes his "identity" being enclosed, surrounded by, created in and through the active statement-events that locate him but over which he exercises no control. Damiens seems pathetic, yet Foucault will show that he is not without power. The forms of power fluctuate, and Damiens is caught within that potential as well as its instability. Damiens is at once a body and a site; he is the material statement of the moment

2 Kantorowitz, *The King's Two Bodies.*

that positions a horizon of statements, a space in his archive, where reversals in the sense of his execution can reconfigure meaning. Foucault gives us the story of Damiens not for dramatic effect, though it certainly has this, but as a demonstration of the problem of genealogy.

Robert-François Damiens attempted to assassinate Louis XV in 1757. Foucault found the record of these gruesome events in the archives of La bibliothèque nationale in Paris.[3] He relays how Damiens was taken to the foot of the main door of the Church of Paris to confess his sorry crime, how he was then delivered in a horse-drawn cart to the site of the execution while being forced to hold aloft a torch of burning wax that would shortly be poured out upon him, how atop a scaffold his flesh was torn apart by hot pincers while molten lead and the melted wax mixed with sulphur were emptied over his wounds, and how finally Damiens was drawn and quartered – an act that necessitated additional horses and a knife to liberate his stubborn limbs from the trunk of his body – until at last Damiens' body was delivered to the stakes to be burned.

The references to the sites of execution (the church, the cart, the scaffold), to excessive torture, and to the body of the wretched Damiens are telling. Damiens is the object of wrath. He is a disobedient body who dared to threaten, and then in turn was afflicted to demonstrate, the sovereign power of Louis XV. In the course of his execution, taken from one public place to another, Damiens exhibits his utter subjugation. His personal body is displaced to become the location of the king's (political) body and the expression of the king's (political) self-control. Sovereignty is played out by pomp. It necessitates a public show, a constant rehearsal of reassurances of and then reinforcements for its domination. Foucault indicates that it was not the crime particularly that attracted royal attention. Indeed, it was not even a display of justice that mattered all that much. Rather, it was the ideal opportunity to demonstrate a royal "dignity" beyond reproach. As Foucault states, "the public execution did not re-establish justice; it reactivated power."[4] It is the site of a sovereign "subjectivity" that Damiens cannot have. The sovereign enacts truth as an exercise of power – as obvious, as flamboyant, as

3 He may have known the story through Baudelaire. See Miller, *The Passion of Michel Foucault*, 225.

4 Foucault, *Discipline and Punish*, 49.

spectacle. And Damiens, reduced to the sympathy of gathered on-lookers, holds power only by way of popular disgust.

In a scene where the absolute royal subject transfers the full weight of its body onto a minor site of resistance, Foucault is able to draw out and present all the spaces of the archive: collateral, correlative, and complementary space. In the reader's encounter with the desperate fate of Damiens, Foucault opens genealogical relationships that account for archival formations. The body of Damiens is a material statement. It demonstrates, effectively hosts, the reasoning of torture. Damiens locates and displays the *episteme* of the present – the there-being of torture – that justifies his having to suffer. The statement-event collapses upon him, yet even for poor Damiens there is on the periphery of his cries a horizon where differently ordered statement-events can elude even kings.

Collateral space, as we have seen, defines two features. One is the competition of space in relation to statements, and the other the ability of statements to shift the order of space. The body of Damiens, as Foucault narrates, is such a location of competition and shifting. In the reasoning of torture lie several competing spaces of the "there." One is surely the ceremony of sovereignty; a second, its physical locations (the church and town square); and a third unfurls in the carnival atmosphere that was always at the fringe of a public execution.

> It was evident that the great spectacle of punishment ran the risk of being rejected by the very people to whom it was addressed. In fact, the terror of the public execution created centres of illegality: on execution days, work stopped, the taverns were full, the authorities were abused, insults or stones were thrown at the executioner, the guards and the soldiers; attempts were made to seize the condemned man, either to save him or to kill him more surely; fights broke out, and there was no better prey for thieves than the curious throng around the scaffold. But above all – and this was why these disadvantages became a political danger – the people never felt closer to those who paid the penalty than in those rituals intended to show the horror of the crime and the invincibility of power.[5]

The wrath poured out on Damiens reveals spaces of competition where we can see the locations of unexpected reversals on the horizon:

5 Foucault, *Surveiller et punir*, 66 (translation mine).

an execution engenders liberty; horror provokes compassion; abuse raises a cry for reform. Contrary to the sovereign effort to exhibit control, the population takes advantage of a reprieve from daily life. This break from daily life gives to – if not almost forces upon – the occasion of an execution an unsanctioned gathering of popular resistance. There is no better argument for the need to limit the royal ego than the obvious abuses involved in its indulgences. At the horizon of the event, Foucault intimates, lies the undoing of the present archive and the persuasions of a new one. These features are accounted for in the competition of space and the consequent, if unplanned, shifts of space.

Correlative space identifies the pre-forming of events in the archive – for example, the act of letter writing pre-forming the interpretive space of encountering the letter writer. In the Damiens story correlative space lies in the way the body is received within distinctive statement-event clusters. In the ordeal of torture Damiens was within two potential horizons: one was the "there" of sovereign excess on the body and the other was ecclesiastical care over the soul.

Correlative space is expressed in the way that Damiens' crime is "fore-given" (pre-formed or pre-interpreted) in the statement-events that receive it. Damiens is obviously fore-given to the royal identity or, as Foucault preferred, the king's two bodies. There is a reading of crime in the statement of the king's body. However, Damiens still lives when the Christian faith permeated the culture of Western Europe, so his crime is likewise fore-given in the church, which is indicated in the very language and spaces employed such as the "*amend honorable*" that is given at the "door of the cathedral." While both locations – royal and religious – correlate statements over the same act of attempted assassination, it can be noted that the reading of the archive (the fore-give-ness of it) is an event of different identities: the executioner and the priest. One extracts vengeance on behalf of the royal body, and the other offers consolation and opportunities to confess. These two correlates are virtually complementary, united in a style of reasoning. The king in the Middle Ages, after all, holds office by divine right, and the church as such represents the metaphysical justification of the social order. The church offered consolation as a type of descending mercy whose place is beside, but not in contradiction to, the king. *Discipline and Punish* does not explore this church and state relationship, though it may be a concern in the unpublished fourth volume of the *History of Sexuality*. For the moment my point is simply to see distinctive correlative spaces operating over the body of Damiens.

A few generations later (1840) virtually the same crime of attempted assassination, this time involving Louis Philipe, the so-called bourgeois king, merited a notably different punishment. The culprit in question was a man named Fieschi, but the act in question demanded not the bodily *amend honorable* that had crushed Damiens but the eyes of a judiciary who would weigh the state of Fieschi's mind in the balances of criminology. Whereas Damiens was the condemned, Fieschi was the criminal; and whereas Damiens was punished in ceremony, Fieshci was judged under the gaze of experts. As Foucault observes, by the early nineteenth century, questions of crime and criminality involve the standard of law and the problem of its dispensation. "Above all," Foucault relays, "no crime committed must escape the gaze of those whose task it is to dispense justice."[6] And a little later, "what was now beginning to emerge was a modulation that referred to the defendant himself, to his nature, to his way of life and his attitude of mind, to his past, to the 'quality' and not the intention of his will."[7]

In this shift from torture to judgment, complementary space comes to the fore. Here the tension between things and words – the office and the speaker or the texture of authority and its performance – is evident. One can note how Damiens and later Fieschi occupy discursive and non-discursive formations. In the case of Damiens, we can focus on the institution of the monarchy and the reasoning of torture. For Fieschi, the diagonal relation that Deleuze would have us imagine stands between the material statement found in a new juridical body and the statement-events that express a new reasoning of justice. Between these two statement formations there exists a tragic association. While one cannot conclude that sovereignty necessarily means torture or a jury necessarily means justice, once set in motion the relationship between these two forms of the statement, a statement-thing and a statement-event, displays a type of *danse macabre*. The material reality of the sovereign requires forms of rebellion over against which "sovereignty" is expressed. The material jury needs a "case" by which to determine criminality. The complement between material statements and statement-events is of tragic proportions. Material statements and statement-events presuppose each other and

6 Foucault, *Discipline and Punish*, 96.
7 Ibid., 99.

often feed off one another. When Foucault claims that there is no better place to learn criminality than in the prison, he invokes this tragic tautology. In effect, the prison produces the reasoning for the need of its own existence. I will explore this subtle dance later by introducing the "echo effect" of the archive.

POWER AS THE PRESENT

The preceding analysis in terms of collateral, correlative, and complementary space serves, at this point, three functions. One is to remind us that the concept of an archive is a spatial rather than theoretical dynamic. An expression of knowledge or a claim of truth, in Foucault, is always a location within relationships more than a reference to an object or a signification of meaning. Second, it highlights power as the key element to understanding what is at stake in the description of spatial relationships. Power is, first, productivity. It works through statement-events to produce (construct) the instant of the event. Second, power explains why the play between the material statement and the statement-event is not casual but vibrant or dynamic. These two elements of power – production and vibrancy – allow a third function to the analysis, which is to show how the archive always involves completion. Archives not only stage the association of spaces but equally display the competitive instability of spaces at the horizon. An archive event opens the operating *episteme* and simultaneously opens a site of epistemic reversal. The archive is the order of things, provided that by such an expression we include the factors of spatiality, power dynamics, and competitive relations.

Such factors are preliminary considerations that set up the much more difficult question of how the experience of meaning is a fabricated event in an archive, a question that involves Foucauldian descriptions of the seeing and the stating of knowledge. Yet this question cannot be approached before it is firmly established that power is not the influence of x upon y but the constitution of the present (the "there-being") of the archive.

Foucault's discussion of the monarchical and juridical archives makes clear that the question whether the material statement or the statement-event is prior cannot be answered. Instead, the two aspects of the statement are understood to be simultaneous. The material statement of the institution of monarchy and the statement-events related to its order of governance form, each to the other, *the neces-sary epistemic presuppositions in the reasoning of monarchical power*. This is explicitly the case when Foucault claims that the re-assertion of the king's power rather than the re-establishment of social order was the aim of Damiens' execution. My point here is to recognize that events in archives must occur as, and really cannot occur other than as, *ap-prehensible* events. The re-assertion of power presumes a relation be-tween act and reason that must be comprehensible or credible in the archive of appearance. Statements and power are the vehicles by which the credible moment is defined, by which it is the "now," the there-being, of the archive. To agree with Foucault that truth and knowledge are fabrications of power in the archive is not to express in sophisticated language a general sense of cynicism, but to acknow-ledge a profoundly penetrating analysis of the texture of a system of reasoning. Thus statement-events imply a whole environment of ap-paratuses (of material statements) that are necessarily involved in the possibility of credible reasoning and acting. "Credible" is shorthand for a unified moment, the now of perception, the form of thought, the stating and the seeing in the archive.

The task at hand, then, is to take Foucault one step further by recog-nizing that spaces of credibility in the archive are spaces of permission. Though this is not a Foucauldian term, it proves constructive when contemplating the located "now" in the archive and its relationship to the horizon. Credible reasoning, such as those forms involved in the monarchical justification of torture, involves "permissible" forms of reason, of course, but the crucial point is that the archive as a whole, in the flux of relationships that compose it, permits a certain reading of the world. Power and the forms it uses permit certain spaces of rea-son and certain systems of reason to operate in credible spaces and credible systems. When the structure of power changes, the permis-sion – the openings available to credible reason – equally shifts.

When the permission to torture, accordingly, shifted from the monarchical archive to the juridical archive, the status of torture changed from punishment to inhumanity: torture no longer made good sense. Thus we can say that permission indicates the persuasion of power working within the order of the archive. Second, permission identifies certain, if limited, boundary activities that function on the edge of the archive. Credible events on the archive boundary remain restricted in potential by the permission or hold of the present. As

Foucault was able to demonstrate, the juridical horizon was always at the edge of the practices of the monarchy. The ceremonies of execution constantly enabled the question of limits to the power of the king. But as such the horizon is not an open field. The juridical archive was a potential archive limited in form by the present space of events. It is extremely significant that permission defines the archival limitation of power on the horizon and that power is not a purely chaotic activity.

To understand the archive genealogically, then, is to understand the sense in which power penetrates and forms the present archive through material statements and statement-events; second, it is to understand that this activity accounts for shifts in the texture of meaning and thus accounts for the permitted emergence of a new archival order. Power is not a force that inhibits or prevents. It is the activity of producing forms that stand in the archive as the objects of desire and that escape the archive as permitted reformations.

> Power would be a fragile thing if its only function were to repress, if it worked only through the mode of censorship, exclusion, blockage and repression, in the manner of a great Superego, exercising itself only in a negative way. If, on the contrary, power is strong this is because, as we are beginning to realize, it produces effects at the level of desire and also at the level of knowledge. Far from preventing knowledge, power produces it.[8]

The archive is not an enclosure but a display, not a mechanism but a permission that composes as equally as it permits credible formations of power. It forms the present in the material event and the statement-event. These express the constructing relationships of power. Now the question is, How are present moments in the archive fabricated as locations of knowledge?

8 Foucault, *Power/Knowledge*, 59.

4

Visibles and Articulables:
A Philosophy of the Event

THE WORLD THAT IS SPOKEN is the articulable world; the world that is seen is the visible world. Articulables and visibles construct the world of experience and are its mode of expression.[1] In both worlds there exists a *constriction of possibility*: events and their interpretation are limited to what the epistemological space of the archive can tolerate. In both worlds there is a *horizon*, which stands at the limit of the archive and restricts the *potential* experience of the event. The epistemic moments of human experience lie within the archive and between the relationship of articulables and visibles.

Despite the similarity of definition, however, the relationship between the articulable world and the visible world is one of competition (Deleuze says, "heterogeneous"[2]). "A battle" defines the juxtaposition of one over against the other and "struggle" describes their mutual association. Foucault ventures little beyond this brief explanation,[3] and

---

1 Deleuze's reflections draw from, but re-interpret, the work of linguist Louis Hjelmslev and apply the insights to Foucault. Deleuze chooses the terms "visibiles" and "articulables" to expand the notion of the strata or formations of history. "Visible" is sometimes a misleading term because it cannot be reduced to "seeing" strictly speaking. It refers to the manner in which content is open to display, as for example in the prison or the clinic. But as "opening to display" it is also, accordingly, hearing, touching, smelling, etc. as much as it is seeing. For futher reference, see Hjelmslev, *Prolegomena to a Theory of Language*.

2 Deleuze, *Foucault*, 66.

3 One will not find in Foucault something beyond the visible and the articulable as modes of dispersion (for example in *Raymond Roussel, The Archaeology of Knowledge*, and *The History of Sexuality*) or as the epistemic circulation of knowledge (*Discipline and Punish*). My development of the problem takes its lead from Deleuze and rests on reflections about light and language in the Panopticon.

the consequence is a lacuna in his argument between the examination of language and light (articulables and visibles) and epistemic events in the archive. I want to show that what can be called "normal" experience in the archive is carved out in the battle between the articulable and the visible.[4]

The relationship between articulables and visibles produces an epistemology or order of knowing the "normal" and thus has a "normalizing effect" that expresses – indeed, that *is* – power in the archive. The normal and the normalizing effect show that in the war Foucault describes, visibles cannot win; equally, the normal and the normalizing effect demonstrate that the consequence of the dominance of the articulable is the experience of "necessity," which I will relate to teleology, in the archive.[5] These analyses add another dimension to Foucault's thought and provide a path for presenting experience in the archive as a hermeneutical problem.

SEEING AND SAYING

What makes up the articulable and visible worlds? Beyond what we say and what we see, or rather in order to speak and to see, what elements function to create these possibilities? In each world there is, first, the condition of existence for the element and second, the conditional setting in which the element is present. The "condition of existence" is linked to space – to how the archive is occupied (its order or constriction) – and the "conditional setting" is linked to potential (horizon) – to how the elements of language and light are present in the archive. "Constriction" and "horizon" are the two key words when it comes to the question of the articulable and visible.

The condition of existence for the articulable is language, and the condition of existence for the visible is light. Language and light are the requirements of existence in each world. One finds here in Foucault perhaps the only retreat, however circuitous it may be, to Kant. Foucault must posit the condition of each world a priori. Yet,

4 The normal archive experience, for the moment, can be understood as an event that is stable and that consequently forms part of the everyday epistemological pattern of the archive operation.

5 The reader will note I am not saying that a particular archive, such as the classical one, is some type of necessary stage in the broader scheme of history; rather, I am saying that necessity is an epistemological experience within an archive.

Foucault's a priori is distinct. In Kant, space and time are a priori in relation to knowledge. Both human perception and human comprehension are given as already using (already engaging in the act of being present by) space and time. In Kant, human experience presumes the fact of space and time. In Foucault, space and time are not categories but fictions: they are fabrications or "effects" of the condition of articulation and light. I begin, then, with an explanation of the fiction of space and time in order to move away from a Kantian and toward a Foucauldian sense of the articulable and visible a priori.

The greatest difficulties are overcome when the Kantian sense of absolute space is recognized as false security.[6] This recognition comes with the affirmation that space cannot be less than "apprehensibility"; that is to say, it cannot be approached as other than rational. Such argumentation may initially seem obscure, for how can it be claimed that space is always rational when Foucault is the author of *Madness and Civilization?* Is not space simply the bland environment in which both reason and unreason are projected? But let us be clear that in the juxtaposition of madness and civilization Foucault intends to describe the "order" (reason) of madness – its imagined or epistemic reality – in the classical (Enlightenment) archive. Space is not posited as an absolute setting hovering behind the scenes. Rather, space is epistemic: it is not the neutral a priori behind order but the very experience of order. Space already always belongs to an order of reason, to the juxtapositions and arrangements of things. Space is not the appearance of things but the order of things. With Foucault, there is no travelling behind the scene to reach an isolated, necessary universal. Space is already the order of the present; it is already the epistemic condition in which such suppositions make sense.

Space is interpretation. It is hermeneutics. It is observation by way of participation. A reach to the foundation or depth of things is always and inevitably the act of engaging the present order of reason. In Foucault, accordingly, space is fundamentally "historicity" – the inescapable hermeneutical condition of being present in the archive.

---

6 In the argument that follows, one might interject that even the "apprehensibility of space" presupposes the fact of space. This can be granted, but it remains impossible to make such a claim "uninterpreted." This is in fact consistent with Kant, who upheld that space is only available to human experience phenomenally. Foucault takes that insight further by socializing space, by unpacking the manner in which power relations, through institutions and technologies, produce the phenomenal experience.

Kant neither realized nor escaped historicity, and so his sense of the
a priori presupposes the reasoning of his own archive. Foucault
knows he cannot escape, and he doesn't bother trying. He knows he
cannot be "outside" the archive that enables his own archaeological
analysis.[7] What he can do is realize his situation. In place of seeing
the great resolution or radical new insight, Foucault opens in his analysis of light and language an avenue along which to examine the
production of space as order and meaning. His question does not
concern space per se but the fabrication of its experience.

In the archive, space (as the order of experience) is produced by
articulation. Or, put in another way, articulables create the condition
of their own emerging exteriority. This means that the articulable
employs the order of an archive when it emerges (even, in order to
emerge) in the statement. Since the statement is the locator of the
archive *episteme*, we must say that the articulable has its exterior (its
condition of existence) by way of the statement. This has two preliminary implications. The first is that articulables, as the surface of the
archive, rest on the accomplishment of the statement (the *statement-
event*). The second is that articulables fabricate social meanings in the
archive because they manifest the relationship of statements, i.e., the
epistemic contours, in the archive. Here then the most difficult point
is made. Since articulables manifest the statement-event (are the exterior of the statement-event accomplishment), they are the evidence
of an order of productivity. Since (on the level of the archive) space
is the epistemological order of experience, articulables express the
condition of possibility for space. In the archive, articulables make
the experience of the exterior order possible; and it is the "making
possible" of the exterior that accounts for the understanding of space
as a fiction produced by the statement. In Foucault, the order of things
is fictional in the sense that there is no absolute foundation, but also
in the sense that order is space produced by means of the statement.

When "time" is placed in this matrix, similar conclusions can be
drawn. Like Kant, Foucault sees space as given prior to time, but for
Foucault time is determined actively (as product) rather than passively (as category). The activity of creating exteriority, which is the
product of articulables, includes the succession of events. Indeed, in
the archive, one can speak of a characteristic age only because one can

7 For example, see note 4 of chapter one.

speak of the successful repetition of an epistemological order across a panorama of events. Time is in this fashion embedded in the archive as the character of repetition and the normalizing influence of repetition within an archive order. The "timetable," which is of great significance in *Discipline and Punish*, is a noteworthy example. The timetable deliberately fabricates an experience of repetition within an order of space (in this case, repeated functions of labour). Each succeeding event is the copy of the event immediately prior; thus, repetition stabilizes the series as "normal" functions. A mechanism such as a timetable, by means of its regulating activity, fabricates a particular experience of the "normal" and, by the act of reproduction, establishes that normal as the grounding justification of further successions.

Following from these two insights, that space is a product of statements and that the succession of events in space (time) accounts for the experience of the normal, it can be concluded that articulables in the archive are a priori both to space (since they are necessary for its production by means of the statement) and to time (since only by means of production is repetition possible). Articulables in consequence are the "form" of archive space according to the statements that expose them, and articulables are the time of experience according to the successful repetition of statements. Again, in another way, articulables are the *constriction of possibility* for the experience of space and time in an archive. They are the necessary components of an operating fiction.[8]

Articulables are evidently active, in relation to space and time, since their activity constantly produces space and time; by contrast visibles (what is seen) are passive, since their activity is the reception of light in an already accomplished archive. Visibles cannot produce light, but they tolerate light as the revelation of their presence, their "here-now."[9]

---

8 The sense of a priori in Foucault is very similar to Heidegger. Here again, from the point of view of Kant, one might stress that space and time must already operate in order for articulables to surface; but for both Heidegger and Foucault it is not possible to arrive at this pre-conceptual level except by what is already given in articulables, which means that the a posteriori condition (the historicity) is already conceptuality itself.

9 Deleuze seems to disagree with this point, for he claimed that visibles are not passive but are rather of a heterogeneous realm. Nevertheless, he concludes that visibles are "not primary," which accounts for the fact that they are "determinable" by the activity of articulables. I have chosen to argue that what is neither primary nor autonomous is passive insofar as its form is determined in the activity that exposes it (see Deleuze, *Foucault*, 60–9).

Just as articulables are the external form of the statement, visibles are the external form of light. Visibles can describe the path light will follow or the line of vision light will traverse according to the order of experience already accomplished in the archive. Thus, while light is the condition of visibles, it does not determine what is seen; or, while light is necessary to seeing, it does not determine the experience of seeing. On the contrary, visibles function to reveal how light is dispersed in the order of the archive. Further, since dispersion is a passive activity, its functional presence shows what the archive tolerates as "normal"; in other words, visibles demonstrate what has already been accomplished in the statement. This is so because dispersion can operate only in the *already-made-exterior* articulable events. The most explicit example of this is the Panopticon, which will be detailed later. For the moment the point is to recognize that the revealing function of light and the producing function of language are the passive and active elements of an archive.

THE STATEMENT AS NORMALIZING EFFECT

Deleuze calls visibles and articulables the "there-is" (and "there-being") of light and language.[10] Articulables function by means of language. Language, Deleuze indicates, is the "there-being" of articulables; language is the manner of "being-at-hand-in-the-world" for articulables. Except for the contrast of passivity and activity, the parallel is exact for light. Visibles function by means of light; light is the "there-being" of visibles (the manner of "being-at-hand-in-the-world").[11] Each instance of "there-being" is also an instance of an appearance of constricted possibility; each "appearance" is already within the condition of possibility in terms of its being seen or being said. Constricted possibilities compose the "conditional setting" of language or light. What then is this conditional setting? One can approach the question by affirming again that statements produce space (or the *epistemic* experience) in which the linguistic act emerges as an event. In this sense, the

---

10 Deleuze, *Foucault*, 58.

11 In Heidegger the *Lichtung* (clearing) is the at-hand disclosure of the spatiality of the "there"; in Foucault, the "there" is a mode of being-there, i.e., an epistemic actuality in the already operating archive; second, the realms of the visible and the articulable are in competitive relation, as we shall see, and the former is not simply available to the latter.

statement is self-referential for the statement is composed of language but at the same time it is the condition of linguistic acts. Thus the statement is *always the absolute presence of the archive as experience.* It is the condition of its own being. But when articulable forms emerge in the archive they can do so only at a location and inside a setting. What is unique about Foucault is that he adds power to the equation. Power circulates in the archive through statements as the relationship of forces – even a regime of forces – that define the setting in which an event will emerge. Statements produce space, but in this act they participate in defining the productivity of an archive's regime of forces. The conditional setting, therefore, is the location of the statement in relation to a productive regime of forces called an archive.

Because the subject here is fundamentally *valeur*, or value, a brief return to structuralism is helpful. Saussure, following Taine, called the diachronic (horizontal) relationship of words "value." A word holds value, whether culturally or historically, because it has a position in relation, within a language, to other words. Words carry a weight of value, and that weight is their cultural and historical position within the larger framework of language. What Foucault has done is raise the stakes. Value is not left in abstraction but is located within the social apparatus. And Foucault does not use the word value but "force." In short, forces produce values, which we can understand as strategic positions in the archive field; values are the experiential effects of the relationship of forces involved in fabricating the moment in an archive. To say that the statement is self-referential because it produces the space of its own appearance, is to draw attention to the manner in which articulables are the simultaneous conjunction of the statement and the dispersion of forces. Articulables imply in their appearance a setting in the archive that tolerates a specific epistemic formation. Another way to say this is that the archive setting is, in the phenomenological sense, the *Lichtung* or "opening" of events according to the manner in which forces have produced the location. Or again, statements produce space but not simply space alone; they produce locations of value according with the matrix of the relationship of forces. In Foucault the whole notion of power/knowledge (in which power and knowledge are present simultaneously) rests on this fundamental insight concerning articulables and visibles in the archive.

Still, the conditional setting of language and light (i.e., their forms of constriction) is at variance in terms of their relationship to one another. Between them there is a struggle, a "battle," where lines are crossed and where one will dominate in the relationship to the other.[12] If at the preliminary level they are identical as conditions, as the "there-being" of language or light, at the level of the conditional setting the relationship is played out as heterogeneous and competitive. The there-being of the articulables is "present" by means of language, and language is infinite; the there-being of visibles is light, and light as receptive is dependent. This fundamental difference is of comprehensive significance because it gives the advantage to language; the consequence is that articulables dominate visibles to the point that visibles replicate the "normal" the articulables have established.

If the world of the articulable is spontaneous and active by reason of its being the condition of language, the world of the visible is receptive and passive by reason of its being the condition of light. What is visible is "produced" passively by the reception of light. Consider a simple object. First the object receives light cast on its form and refracts that light; then, a viewer receives the refraction of light to experience the form of the object. Due to this fundamental dependence on "reception" in order to be "event," the condition of light is defined as passive. The contrast with articulables touches several points: the act of being exterior for the visible is the act of the receptivity of light; visibles are not locations that emerge in the production of constriction but rather depend on the accomplishment of constriction to be seen. Deleuze calls visibles "flashes of light" that reveal an already constricted event. In effect, the "event" that has already taken place linguistically predetermines (holds), on behalf of the visible, the revealing location of space. Thus the statement, in the act of producing space, is a priori to the visible act of revealing space. In this way, the statement can be called a determining form, for it composes the *episteme* in which forces flow and events emerge, whereas the visible is a determined form, for it is present only by receiving light on what has already been given. Because of this difference, Deleuze explains, "We can assume that determination always comes from the statement."[13]

Deleuze, however, by leaving the matter here, stops short of the most important question. Though the statement is determining in its relation to the visible, is it not correct to express that domination as

12　Deleuze, *Foucault*, 68.
13　Ibid., 67.

"interpretation"? The statement, in its engagement of the relationship of archival forces, "allows" or "tolerates" the reception of light according to the *order of location* it has actively opened. In the battle between the two worlds, then, "light-being" is dominated by the interpretation of "language-being." "Light" in effect is the colonial frontier of language; light is won over by interpretation. How is this so?

At the point of light reception, the active agent (the statement) establishes the "constriction of possibility" before the passive agent can appear as an event. Thus, the statement has already dominated the visible as interpretation before the visible can surface as an event. The statement's effect on the visible is accordingly "normality"; the statement is the setting (the opening) of the constriction of possibility *already achieved* in the world of the articulable. Light-being has its "presence," is an actual occasion, by means of the event (the standard, the measure) already achieved in the statement. Consequently, the effect of the event of the statement in its battle with the visible is called the "normalizing effect" because it constricts the visible according to the order of the articulable; or, it creates the possibility of "presence" for the visible by means of the accomplishment of the articulable. This significant consideration, surprisingly not addressed by Deleuze, irresistibly leads to examining the visible as the repetition of the articulable.

Repetition at the level of the visible shows how in the reception of light the accomplishment of the statement is repeated or reinforced. The visible is dominated because its effect, accordingly, is to support the statement, to be its opening, and to be its evidence. This repetition can be described as an echo. In its condition of existence, the visible repeats the accomplishment of the statement-event: it echoes in an act of reinforcement the interpretation already achieved in the archive by the statement. Though this description is found neither in Deleuze nor Foucault, it is useful because it can address the problem both authors leave in silence, which is the hermeneutical problem of a "normalizing effect" in the archive. The unassuming image of an echo successfully identifies this effect.

An "echo" occurs when the product of the statement is repeated in the form of the visible. The echo accordingly is the evidence of the statement. But more importantly, in this act, it places a "hold" on the horizon of the archive; an echo reinforces a disposition or expectation toward the horizon. It tames, as it were, the potential of the succession of events. When it is said that the "echo" thereby places a hold on the horizon, what is meant is that the echo *reinforces the anticipation* of successive events. As we shall see in the case of the Panopticon, the act of enclosing the body in a cell for the purposes of discipline is an epistemological accomplishment of archive statements. The act of "enclosing" is an "acting out" of the reasoning or, better, the order of reason in an archive. But the act of enclosing is equally an order of vision that repeats, in the visual lines of the relationship, what is "normal knowledge" according to the epistemic order. Thus in the moments that pass, in the succession of events, between the observer and the imprisoned body a structure of "seeing" both underlines and anticipates the next event. The visibles as the echo of the statement place in the archive a weight on the horizon. The constant repetition of the statement in the echo re-interprets the order of succession as the normal flow of experience.

More than merely repeating in the visible form what is achieved in the statement form, the echo effectively reinforces an order of reasoning. Its continuous repetition is a "normalizing effect" because succeeding events are anticipated according to the echo already established in the statement-event.

Foucault's great example, the Panopticon, demonstrates how the echo works.

5

The Panopticon:
Technology of an Accomplished Archive

UNDER, IF NOT IN CONTENTION WITH, the ostentatious and cruel punishments of Louis XV's regime lay the variable forces of what Foucault called the "juridical" archive. While public executions were often accompanied by the enthusiasm of the masses, we have seen that there always remained another side to the story. Public executions created spaces of reversal, as Foucault astutely noticed, where the intentions of the monarch more or less backfired. The crowd could judge a criminal penalty unjust. Riots rather than awe could be the consequence. The potential of social unrest, even as onlookers stood in silence, lurked in the background. An execution could inadvertently facilitate the moment of resistance. "Preventing an execution, that was regarded as unjust, snatching a condemned man from the hands of the executioner, obtaining his pardon by force, possibly pursuing and assaulting the executioners, in any case abusing the judges and causing an uproar against the sentence – all this formed part of the popular practices that invested, traversed and often overturned the ritual of the public execution."[1]

This site of potential resistance running concurrently with the official execution of justice is one particularly identifiable place where a reversal stirs in an archive. In this case excessive punishment opened a type of archival permission to classical reformers who, as Foucault describes, raised the question of limits. To what extent is the "king," too, required to observe – rather than to be – the law? The reformers concluded that the violence of the king contradicted the common humanity of individuals. Foucault relays the examples of Jérôme

---

1 Foucault, *Discipline and Punish*, 59–60.

Pétion de Villeneuve, Boucher d'Argis, and Joseph de Maistre. And, as the reader contemplates this basic shift in understanding, it is clear that "humanism" in its modern sense is born on the foundation of a new judiciary process. "The need for punishment without torture was first formulated as a cry from the heart or from an outraged nature."[2] Even more to the point, the cry also afforded the first glimpse at a new regime of power where punishment is measured in relation to the severity of crime. Crime is now placed on a social grid, and the judgments of a jury displace the revenge of a monarch.

Yet, despite this glimpse at a new order, something remains intact. For the reformers, Foucault says, it is not a question of transforming the nature of the criminal but rather of respecting the human being the criminal is. The concern is "not that which must be reached in order to alter him, but that which must be left intact in order to respect him."[3] Foucault insists that the inverse of monarchical sovereignty is the sovereignty of the individual. The eclipse of the monarch is at the same time the birth of "man." This new archive exists only briefly, according to Foucault, at the end of the eighteenth century. He presents it as a stepping-stone between the king's body and the disciplinary society.

Foucault, then, brings the eighteenth century to the fore as if a reflective pause. He dwells on the reformers only to move his reader on to the nineteenth century and the birth of the prison. Of course, the prison has existed in various forms since antiquity. It did not just suddenly appear. But Foucault is right to speak of its nineteenth-century form uniquely as a prison system. Prior to the Enlightenment, a prison, if it could be so called, functioned mainly to hold the accused, usually under great duress, before a punishment was executed. Rarely was a prison imagined or used as the principal means of reform. Thus, in defining a reversal that stands between the monarch and the disciplinary society, Foucault brings our attention immediately to the invasions of a new archival order. It is as if an archive can show cracks before it breaks apart or can have moments of obvious interruption before it resets in the form of a new regime of power. This is history understood as genealogy: there is no hidden teleology at work as Foucault crosses from one regime to another. The quest is to identify

2 Ibid., 74.
3 Ibid.

the locations of transformation. He finds them in these subtle and sometimes strange archival interruptions. Here lies the space where events get caught in the ebb and flow of power and where eventually the statement achieves a new occasion of permission.

Moving from the king's body to the prison takes us through commentary on the "gaze," already defined in Foucault's study of medical perception (see *The Birth of the Clinic*). The gaze successively shifts in the three-step movement from the monarchy, to reform, and then to discipline. It moves from the public spectacle to trained classification, and then from trained classification to professional penetration. After the monarchy, the reforming interest was to classify crime on a scale inclusive of all criminal acts. Each criminal act could be measured in severity against another. Acts measured less serious could satisfy the public debt with less severe punishment, whereas serious acts could merit physical punishment or execution. In this sense, the reformers had a juridical eye, an eye trained to gaze upon crime within the interpretive frame of the social contract. A criminal act was an injury to the social body. Juridical practices employed a system of grading, comparing, and positioning one act within a family of acts. Since criminal acts create disequilibrium in society, the body of the individual criminal becomes a site where the return to balance must be achieved. Foucault particularly points out the recourse to public works in place of ancient methods of torture and shame. So-called chain gangs are examples of forced community service, and in them the criminal body "signs" repentance not as a reformed individual but as the representation of the need to satisfy a public debt. In addition, the very exposure of the criminal publicly expresses both a civic confession of guilt and a warning to society at large. "The guilty person is only one of the targets of punishment. For punishment is directed above all at others, at all the potentially guilty. So these obstacle-signs that are gradually engraved in the representation of the condemned man must therefore circulate rapidly and widely; they must be accepted and redistributed by all; they must shape the discourse that each individual has with others and by which crime is forbidden to all by all."[4]

When Foucault moves on to describe the disciplinary archive, he recounts something of the same motion from monarchical excesses to

4 Ibid., 108.

juridical practices. When the jury delivers the body of the condemned to the public viewing of works, a second regime of power loiters, as it were, at the archive periphery waiting to invade. The brief appearance of the juridical archive was composed of an indecisive mixture of old monarchical power, new juridical measurements, and increasing practices of imprisonment. But it is the prison system that becomes the mainstay. Discipline effectively invades the jury; the gaze that classifies crime now refocuses to judge criminal nature; and as the examination of crime falls more and more into the possession of experts, the debt lies no longer in society but increasingly in the criminal's subjectivity.

In the disciplinary society the need is to reform the self, but in order to satisfy such an ideal the professionals must set the benchmark. Discipline is all about the professional gaze penetrating the criminal personality and determining the agenda of reform. "Criminality" is born as part of the "nature of man" that demands in response a new "science of man."[5] In the disciplinary archive, rather than repaying social debt, punishment aims to correct a subjective deviation; one seeks not "to efface the crime but to transform a criminal."[6] Discipline is punishment understood as training rather than atoning. "The difference is to be found in the procedure of access to the individual, the way in which the punishing power gets control over him, the instruments that it uses in order to achieve this transformation; it is in the relation that it establishes with the body and with the soul, and not in the way that it is inserted within the legal system."[7] A disciplinary gaze is cast not on the body but through it – and by means of it – to hidden motivations, behaviours, and habits. The key image for this new regime of power is the architecture of the Panopticon.

THE PANOPTICON

Foucault discovered the Panopticon in the works of Jeremy Bentham;[8] Bentham for his part gave credit for the discovery to his brother whom he had visited at Crichoff in White Russia in 1786. The

---

5 I say "nature of man" and "science of man" in the spirit of the modern ideal of singular and deep identities. The quotation marks indicate that in our time the expression is judged exclusive and chauvinistic.

6 Foucault, *Discipline and Punish*, 127.

7 Ibid.

8 Recounted in *Power/Knowledge*, 146–7.

Panopticon is not, strictly speaking, a prison design, though it may be best known as such; it is rather a machine of surveillance that stands, in Foucault's mind, at the apogee of the disciplinary society. The Panopticon, as we shall see, is the complement of the plague and the reverse of the dungeon. This novel "device" might first be described in the terse words of Bentham himself:

> The building is circular. The apartments of the prisoners occupy the circumference. You may call them, if you please, the *cells*. These *cells* are divided from one another, and the prisoners by that means secluded from all communication with each other, by *partitions* in the form of *radii* issuing from the circumference towards the centre, and extending as many feet as shall be thought necessary to form the largest dimensions of the cell. The apartment of the inspector occupies the centre; you may call it if you please the inspector's lodge. It will be convenient in most, if not all cases, to have a vacant space or *area* all round, between such centre and such circumference. You may call it if you please the *intermediate* or *annular* area. About the width of a cell may be sufficient for a passage from the outside of the building to the lodge. Each cell has in the outward circumference, a *window*, large enough, to afford light enough to the correspondent part of the lodge. The inner circumference of the cell is formed by an iron *grating* so light as not to screen any part of the cell from the inspector's view ... To the windows of the lodge there are *blinds*, as high up as the eyes of the prisoners in their cells can, by any means they can employ, be made to reach. To prevent thorough light, whereby, notwithstanding the blinds, the prisoners would see from the cells whether or no any person was in the lodge, that apartment is divided into quarters, by *partitions* formed by two diameters to the circle, crossing each other at right angles.[9]

A central tower of observation, around which circle prison cells (conceivably stacked several stories high), hides the eyes of a secretive but constant surveyor. The cells are illuminated, whether by lights or windows in the background, in contrast to the mysterious darkness of the tower. This is a simple architecture that supports multiple effects. The surveying eye is constant, but unverifiable. It issues a concealed but no

9 Bentham, *The Works of Jeremy Bentham*, 40–1.

less intervening force upon an enclosed body. Unlike the transitory yet explosive power of a monarch in former times, this technology relies on minimal forces of permanent consequence. The panoptic sight lines continually fall upon the imprisoned body, silently judging its movements, silently reinforcing an expected standard of behaviour. The "prisoner" is obliged to display, by physical postures, a conforming obedience to an imposed condition of disciplinary self-reflection. The prisoner is challenged to show that in the depths of a secret self the expectations of a watching eye are satisfied. The Panopticon obliges conformity between the centre and the circumference. It places the interior of the prisoner at highest magnitude. The Panopticon searches the hidden self, perhaps the lost self, and its buried motivations; it carefully manufactures the condition of a self-constituted subjectivity, which is the debt returned from the prisoner to the tower. Bentham's brilliance was in conceiving an economy of forces dedicated to implanting social norms into the self-realizing subjectivity of a formerly deviant object. In short, he designed the architecture for creating a soul.

To Foucault, the technology of the Panopticon correlates with and, in a sense, signifies the victory of disciplinary practices that first emerged during the time of the plague. It is not incidental that the section entitled "Panopticism" in *Discipline and Punish* begins with a seventeenth-century description of measures to be taken in a town infested by plague. As an unexpected and nameless catastrophe for which a culprit was constantly sought, the plague brought with it a whole set of social demands that opened new appropriations of space to controlling observations and meticulous government. In contrast to the social "problem" of the leper, who was shuffled off to the outside of society by categorical exclusion, the management of the plague demanded an encompassing and inclusive gaze of simultaneous and indiscriminate activity. It is a gaze most adaptable to a disease of indefinite origin and sweeping occurrence. It is also the gaze of discipline that defines the eye the Panopticon placed in a central tower.

Something as frightening and incomprehensible as the plague demanded the government of individuals on a large scale. Government was exercised not so much through increased bureaucratic structures as through new practices and machines, new regulations to control public space, and new techniques of isolation and partitioning to segregate inflicted individuals. Rather than being ignored by exclusion, the plague victim was literally observed to death.

If it is true that the leper gave rise to rituals of exclusion ... then the plague gave rise to disciplinary projects. Rather than the massive, binary division between one set of people and another, it called for multiple separations, individualizing distributions, an organization in depth of surveillance and control, an intensification and a ramification of power. The leper was caught up in a practice of rejection, of exile-enclosure; he was left to his doom in a mass among which it was useless to differentiate; those sick of the plague were caught up in a meticulous tactical partitioning in which individual differentiations were the constricting effects of a power that multiplied, articulated and subdivided itself; the great confinement on the one hand; the correct training on the other.[10]

Here is Foucault's description of the quarantine practices of a town stricken with plague, on which the above quotation is based:

First, a strict spatial partitioning: the closing of the town and its outlying districts, a prohibition to leave the town on pain of death, the killing of all stray animals; the division of the town into distinct quarters, each governed by an intendant. Each street is placed under the authority of a syndic, who keeps it under surveillance; if he leaves the street, he will be condemned to death ... The syndic himself comes to lock the door of each house from the outside; he takes the key with him and hands it over to the intendant of the quarter; the intendant keeps it until the end of the quarantine. Each family will have made its own provisions; but, for bread and wine, small wooden canals are set up between the street and the interior of the houses, thus allowing each person to receive his ration without communicating with the suppliers and other residents; meat, fish and herbs will be hoisted up into the houses with pulleys and baskets. Only the intendants, syndic and guards will move about the streets and also, between the infected houses, from one corpse to another, the 'crows,' who can be left to die: these are 'people of little substance who carry the sick, bury the dead, clean and do many vile and abject offices.' It is a segmented, immobile,

10 Foucault, *Discipline and Punish*, 198.

ALSO NOT A PUNISHMENT BUT A WAY OF SAVING

YET NOT "OBSERVATION"

frozen space. Each individual is fixed in his place. And, if he moves, he does so at the risk of his life, contagion or punishment.[11]

Not surprisingly, Foucault's association of plague with panopticism has been criticized by several commentators. Is his promotion of the Panopticon as an archetype of social space carried out at the expense of historical accuracy? The question rests on justified suspicion. In truth the Panopticon as a fact exists rarely; the Maison centrale at Rennes in France and the Stateville Penitentiary (which still operates) in Illinois are among the few concrete examples. The criticism is that Foucault has taken the significance of the incidental and delivered it to the height of the incredible. "The analysis of *Discipline and Punish*," according to Jacques-Guy Petit, "presents aspects of reductionism that take no account of the diversity and complexity of the social and ideological game which exists even within bourgeoisie power."[12] But Foucault's position remains defensible. The Panopticon is no blanket attempt to homogenize the middle class. Rather it attempts to represent a problem. Even from the time of his study of the medical gaze, undertaken several years before *Discipline and Punish*, Foucault had noticed how the architectural considerations for the reconstruction of Hôtel-Dieu in 1772 addressed the issue of "visible bodies" and partitioning for "undue contact" to prevent contagion.[13] It is not a question of merely observing these themes and cataloguing them. Foucault understands here how the element of visibility has newly expressed itself as a conceptual desire. Foucault introduces us to a new arrangement of forces, a point Petit seems to miss. Reductionism is indeed an act undertaken to pacify complexity, but the Panopticon is a consequence of forces, and points to them, rather than their pacification. Indeed, the Panopticon is representative of an already complex and active circulation of forces that work precisely to pacify. The Panopticon expresses an epistemic commitment at the level of the disciplinary archive to conformity. This then raises a crucial distinction. In the archive, there is a place to talk about event-emergence, about points of reversal and new orders of the statement. But (as we have seen with visibles and articulables) there

11 Ibid., 197.
12 See Petit, "Le philanthrope et la cité panoptique," *Michel Foucault.*
13 Foucault, *Power/Knowledge*, 146.

is another place to talk about accomplishment. An archive at a certain point can be considered accomplished, meaning that it defines the normative assumptions of epistemic activity, not that it reaches its zenith. The archive is accomplished in effect when it becomes the experiential present. When Foucault speaks of the Panopticon, he is describing an activity of production that is accomplished. Rather than reductive, the analysis of the Panopticon gives to us the social and ideological forces that construct a present-historic experience.

François Ewald understands this subtlety with great clarity. He correctly sees in the Panopticon a mechanism intimately linked to the fabrication of homogenized social spaces, to an accomplishment of reduction that might otherwise be called "normality":

> Foucault did not want to say that the disciplinary society was a society of confinement in general. Actually, he meant the inverse. In effect, the diffusion of the disciplines is manifest proof that their techniques are foreign to the principle of confinement or, more exactly, that with the disciplines confinement is no longer segregation. The characteristic of the disciplinary society is precisely that the disciplines do not enclose. On the contrary, their diffusion, far from splitting up or compartmentalizing society, homogenizes social space. The emphasis in the idea of the disciplinary society is the idea of society itself: the disciplines fabricate society; they create a sort of common language between all sorts of institutions; they make it possible for one to be translated into another.[14]

The Panopticon is architectural technology: it is a mechanism of disciplinary space. The Panopticon is the symbolic characterization of what is already operating as and defining an *episteme*. Therefore, the Panopticon has a basic paradox about it: yes, it is a rather all-inclusive symbol of the disciplinary society that displays mechanisms of enclosure, but the point is that panoptic "enclosures" display spaces of observation, of constricted and trained movements, of "events" within a theatre of contrived meaning. The Panopticon encloses in order to display. When Ewald speaks of homogenization, he speaks of fabricated or produced constrictions. He wants to highlight the panoptic effect of multiple parts observed by the same technical standard. The

14 Ewald, "A Power without an Exterior," *Michel Foucault Philosopher*, 170.

plague is the complement of the Panopticon because both involve the same set of practices; confinement and seclusion used to open the body to general observation and normalizing judgment.

Ewald appropriately asks what constitutes the fundamental texture of the forces of homogenization that renders possible the "interplay of redundant elements and infinite homologies"?[15] Or, if this question can be slightly altered, at what point is an archive accomplished such that the characteristics of its *episteme* become the assumption of its operation and justification of its normalizing regard?

An archive can be considered accomplished when its occupation of space conforms to its statement-events. That is, when what is seen is in effect the product of what is practised then the "normal" has become the assumption of the "present." These words, it is true, can be difficult to decipher, but their intention needs to be clear. *An accomplished archive occurs when the lines of vision repeat the events of the statement.* The Panopticon is so outstanding in its ability to convey this insight that perhaps Foucault's most impressive achievement lies here. The panoptic machinery actively creates *lines of vision* in the way it places a hidden eye over against an exposed body. The body consequently becomes the site of automatic or habitual conformity to the epistemic order of statements that the eye employs to read it. The panoptic eye, which is no less the product of the Panopticon, seeks in and through the secluded body the reproduction of panoptic statements. The Panopticon is the production of an order of perception; it is or, in its accomplishment, becomes the justification of the activity of itself. It is the machine of perpetual motion.

This brings about the second characteristic of an accomplished archive; as normative experience, it no longer has an exterior. This point consists of two decisive elements. First, because the archive itself is a way of seeing, its "exterior" is a hermeneutical experience created from within what is already its "point of view." Or, in a simpler form and in keeping with Foucauldian language, the archive's exterior is an ironic production of its own interior (a thought to be developed later). The second element is that the very deportment of experience in an archive is constantly *reflexive*. I mean by this that an accomplished archive renders itself accountable (returns to or redirects itself) to the order of its central statement-events. These central statement-events

15 Ibid.

can be regarded as its technology. Foucault links the experience of
the normal in the disciplinary archive to three central statement-
events that he calls techniques of accountability: hierarchical surveillance, normalizing judgment, and the examination. Though we need
to appreciate how these techniques function, for the moment the
point is to see them as the *technologies* of discipline.

We are bodies trapped inside minds,[16] Foucault claimed, indicating that the whole effort of *Discipline and Punish* rests on the radical
assertion that disciplinary technologies have the effect of creating a
soul. More than this, disciplinary surveillance also expresses an accomplished archive that emerged along the path of transformation
from the king's body to the tower by means of the jury. The disciplinary soul is a product of these mechanisms; it is the accomplishment
of the Panopticon because it is its repetition. An archive is accomplished when the forms of its statements silently construct the repetitions of its epistemic regime. Accordingly, a most discerning point
will be gained through understanding not only the transition from
one archive to another but also recognizing in this transition lines of
vision come to correlate and complement statement-events.

SURELY. GOD SHOULD BE MENTIONED HERE...

---

16 Foucault, *Discipline and Punish*, 30.

6

Statements and Things:
On the Emergence of Archives

THE PANOPTICON IS RELATED to the juridical archive that preceded it and gave "permission" to its architecture. Precedent archives create the conditions for liminal or counter-archival events that mark in their activity an area of permission (a horizon) for new accomplishments. I have called this area of permission a *constriction of possibility* in the sense that it opens space conditionally related to the productivity of precedent archival forces. But new space can't be simply anything. Rather, the forces of a new epistemic order will in some manner be the product of the older activity: this is why the new space must be understood as a constricted possibility.

A very brief review will serve to orient the new question. How does a precedent archive set a constriction of possibility for a new archive and what does this mean epistemologically when it comes to talking about archive normalcy and standards of truth?

When the conversation is about the inside of an archive, the subject matter is the regulation of events – that is, how events actively form a network of repetition – and how the statement is the manifest location of events. Foucault, we recall, had two senses for the statement: one is related to articulables and it can be called the statement-event; and a second is related to institutions and it can be called the statement-thing. There is also the third element, visibles, but visibles act passively to repeat the accomplishment of the statement. The statement then is actively present in the physics of both articulables and things (things such as architecture, floor plans, etc., but equally governmental bureaucracies, positions of authority, the weight of the expert's voice). When Foucault considers a movement or shift from a precedent archive to a new archive, his concern is with the emergence of a new statement. He does not lead us to monumental personalities who inaugurate historic breakthroughs, like Marx or Freud, except to the degree (as we have seen) that these authors are indeed statement-events that initiate new discursive practices.[1] Rather, concern is focused on discontinuities, transgressions, and reversals in the activity of an archive and on events that signal ruptures, instability, and potential shifts. Accordingly, the practical influence of the statement-event and statement-thing is not only archive-creating and archive-defining but also constitutive of an emerging "present" in the conditions of a new archive broken from its predecessor. In the change from one archive to another, we need to see not modifications or advances in knowledge but the creation of new conditions of reasoning and new senses of being present.

ARCHIVES AS THE ANONYMOUS PRODUCT OF ARCHIVES

In this section, I employ some examples that Foucault uses to demonstrate how peripheral practices can invade, reverse, and reconstitute the *episteme* of a given archive. In each case, the practices of the statement (specifically statement-things) open a space of shifted or reconstructed social aims.

The first example lies in the contrast, briefly mentioned in chapter 3, between the dramatic execution of Damiens and the judgment of insanity placed on Joseph Fieschi. On 28 July 1835, during the fifth anniversary celebrations of the July Monarchy, Fieschi tried, unsuccessfully, to assassinate Louis Philippe. Though Fieschi too was guilty of attempted regicide, his setting is some eighty-three years later than Damiens, and his body, we can recall, is measured differently. Though he faced the same fate, his execution does not involve the public exposure of his body and his suffering but rather the modesty of his body, the hiding of his face, and a death sentence effected immediately without torture. As Foucault relates, "He will be taken to the place of execution wearing a shirt, barefoot, his head covered with a black veil; he will be exhibited upon a scaffold while an usher reads the sentence to the people, and he will be immediately executed."[2]

1 Foucault, "What Is an Author?" Adams and Searle, *Critical Theory Since 1965*, 138–48.
2 Ibid., 13.

In the Fieschi case, the execution is still public but it is not an exhibition. His facial expressions are masked, hiding sensation; the criminal dies almost privately underneath a pall. The crime (publicly recited as the perpetrator's confession) rather than the body takes centre stage, and it is the weight of his soul (his criminal insanity) that is measured in the balances of justice.

Foucault grants that in the nineteenth century the reduction of torture did not mean its disappearance in relation to crime. It still lingers in the Western system, and in any case he speaks of no uniform movement. The stress is on subtle shifts that too often are read as civilized refinements rather than evidence of a change in the architecture of reasoning. "The reduction in penal severity in the last 200 years is a phenomenon with which legal historians are well acquainted. But for a long time, it has been regarded in an overall way as a quantitative phenomenon: less cruelty, less pain, more kindness, more respect, more 'humanity.' In fact these changes are accompanied by a displacement in the very object of the punitive operation."[3] It is this archival *displacement* of body with soul, of the surface with the hidden, that Foucault wants to bring to our attention: "Certainly the 'crimes' and 'offences' on which judgement is passed are juridical objects defined by the [penal] code, but judgement is also passed on passions, instincts, anomalies, infirmities, maladjustments, effects of environment or heredity ... It is these shadows lurking behind the case itself that are judged and punished."[4]

This basic shift from body to soul is to Foucault not only a reorientation and reclassification of the body in the archive but also represents the productive activities of a new *episteme* in which disciplinary training is manufactured as the new ideal. The panoptic society is essentially defined by forces passing through events aimed at training. And Foucault offers several other locations for this phenomenon. Military training is one. Foucault claims that where discipline was once a means to prevent looting and desertion, and thus was a force pressed from top military ranks onto lower ranks, the panoptic shift involves the idealization of discipline as technical skill, self-control, and the virtual effacement of passion. Factories and schools mark another social area of panoptic invasion. "The discipline of the workshop," Foucault

3 Ibid., 16.
4 Ibid., 17.

remarks, "all the while remaining a way of enforcing respect for the regulations and authorities ... tends to increase aptitudes, speeds, output, and therefore profits." The panoptic effect converts the purposes of supervision from the curtailment of laxity to productivity where a worker's aptitude and speed constitute a trained self. And again, "In the seventeenth century, when the provincial schools or the Christian elementary schools were founded, the justifications given for them were above all negative ... Now, at the beginning of the revolution, the goal prescribed for primary education was to be, among other things, to 'fortify,' to 'develop the body,' to prepare the child 'for a future in some mechanical work,' to give him 'an observant eye, a sure hand and prompt habits.'"[5]

These examples of social transformation need to be carefully considered. The first impulse is to recognize that Foucault is describing the flow of power in society and leave it at that. He is after all suggesting that in the juridical archive power descends from above to inhibit the activity of the masses and limit the free expression of individual passions. Its form of production is negative or depressing. Then, from the periphery of this experience, the panoptic ideal invades, moving to and emerging as the centre of a new order. Now power seemingly invests itself in the agent as subjectivity. It becomes that relationship of forces in and through which the individual is fabricated positively as a location of discipline. This is certainly part of the problem displayed in these examples where the Panopticon practically inverts the juridical regard. But the picture is not complete.

In addition, the recognition that in this shifting activity from jury to training, the role of power is constantly ironic is crucial. Though Foucault can describe the juridical space as primarily depressing, restraining, and preventing, this does not mean he regards the flow of power in this archive as strictly negative. In fact power is effectively always positive. Even its negative expression is productive. Power is constantly producing the condition of the statement, and indeed power is the statement or, at the very least, is manifest in the form of the statement. Even to curtail the activity of power is immediately to produce altered arrangements of power. To inhibit stealing in the

---

5 Foucault, *Surveiller et punir*, 212 (translation mine). Foucault took the reference to education from Léon, *La Révolution française et l'éducation technique* (1968). Léon is referring to the *Rapport de Talleyrand à la Constituante, 10 septembre 1791*.

army is to produce a space permitting surveillance; to inhibit school children from copying is to produce a space permitting individual achievement. The negative expression of power remains equally and ironically positive since it is still the act of setting archival permission. "What makes power hold good," Foucault says, "what makes it ac-cepted, is simply the fact that it doesn't only weigh on us as a force that says no, but that it traverses and produces things, it induces pleasure, forms knowledge, produces discourse."[6]

A second element to emphasize is the anonymity of the activity of power. Power is present consistently in the circulation of statements that create the conditions of possibility in an archive, but the very consistency of power is exactly the factor of instability. One event of the statement in one epistemic formation of an archive can quickly reverse. What the statement-event permits is curiously dualistic. A statement-event opens the epistemic performance of an archive, but immediately in this act it opens to itself, at its own horizon, the re-verse of itself. Thus, to the extent that the statement-event belongs to the particular space of one epistemic formation, it is a "constricted" event, but in the sense that the statement-event also opens a space of reversal on the back of its own constriction, it permits the presence of a shift in formation. In this way, an archive rather anonymously pro-duces an archive (an "other" archive) by producing the forces of its own displacement.

If, then, discipline is taken as an event of constriction at the horizon of juridical practices, the emergence of discipline is not a case of as-cending development but of descending genealogy. If it were strictly a question of progress to higher stages of development, Foucault would have to resort to other techniques; he would be obliged to introduce the great innovators of the past; he would need to recall particular moments of crises and resolutions; he would have to be a "historian" of ideas and culture; he might even talk of a paradigm shift. From the reader's point of view, he would have to provide something more than the apparent "heightened effects" and "before and after snap-shots" that both mark and hide larger complexities.[7] But the genea-logical question is set on another footing: it is not a general account *of* what happened; it is rather an accounting of the *experience* of what

---

6 Foucault, *Power/Knowledge*, 119.
7 See Hacking, *Foucault: A Critical Reader*, 29.

happened. Genealogy is not about history, at least not directly, but about the imagination of the present. Even more to the point, it is the act of comprehending how *what happened* was experienced as meaning according to an archive's functioning regime of truth and its active network of power. What mechanisms can account for the spatiality of truth, its forms of constriction, and event locations? What sets of practices account for "the gradual extension of the mechanisms of discipline throughout the seventeenth and eighteenth centuries, their spread throughout the whole social body," and "the formation of what might be called in general the disciplinary society"?[8]

With the Panopticon Foucault offers no history of prisons but rather an account of an emerging constriction of possibility whose product is the humanist subject. He displays here the defining relationship of forces that involves architectures, lines of vision, instrumentality, timetables, and targets. What we are dealing with, Foucault declares, "is a 'physics' or an 'anatomy' of power, a technology."[9] Panopticism is not to be reduced to bureaucracy or dismissed as institutionalization. Panopticism is not one function of power but a modality of power. It is a productive constriction of possibility. It is the manufacturing of the present. In other words, the Panopticon is to be examined genealogically as space.

INSIDE THE PANOPTICON

Archives emerge from the peripheries of preceding practices, but if they are to remain in place there needs to be an element of stability. That element is repetition.[10] Insofar as the circulation of power can reproduce the statement, an archive remains in place as the epistemic foundation of the present.

The Panopticon is the supreme machine of repetition. Inside, a subject is isolated in a cell and looks out on a strikingly obvious yet mysteriously obscured tower. From the tower a surreptitious gaze returns to the subject. Whether or not the tower is occupied, the subject in the cell is under permanent surveillance. From the cell to the

---

8 Foucault, *Discipline and Punish*, 209.

9 Ibid., 215.

10 Here again one must rely on Deleuze who sometimes understood Foucault better than Foucault did. See Deleuze, *Difference and Repetition*.

tower a line of vision travels clearly, directly, to the furtive gaze of the tower's occupant. With equal ease, from the tower a gaze returns again. It can be said that the lines of vision cast from the cell hit the tower only to turn back, to reflect or echo. The vision of the subject in the cell becomes a self-inflicted gaze, a subjectivity. In the Panopticon, self-observation is the fate of every cell.

The tower's surreptitious production of a gaze (for while the tower is seen the gaze from it is not) is cast not just on the body but also on its gestures. Movements signify obedience. The hours of waking and sleeping, the habits of eating and praying, the acknowledgment of limits, and the recognition of rules all reveal a trained and submissive spirit. The panoptic gaze is a gaze into the interior of a subject. It breaks beneath the skin. It seeks human nature. But here is the catch: human nature is its permission; it is the panoptic statement-event. Lines of vision in the Panopticon only re-enforce what is already accomplished in its architecture and what is already the definition of its reasoning. Hence the Panopticon is the machine of discipline. Its unique design portrays the permission of self-actualized subjectivity. It displays how discipline succeeds by disappearing, by receding into the body to become the mind. In the Panopticon subjectivity is produced as the object of desire.

Lines of vision return faithfully and permanently from the tower to the cell. Aside from the constant production of subjectivity there remains one more effect. The tower sits before the subject as its norm. The subject must ingest the normalcy of the tower's gaze. The Panopticon produces a normal standard, but this becomes the sounding stone of the disciplinary self. In effect, the normal is what can be reproduced, repeated, such that it silently enters the presuppositions of archival experience. At this level of tacit operation, where the subject's expectations are born within the forces of epistemic habit, an echo in the lines of vision can be identified. An archive echo rebounds in the subtle repetitions, re-enforcements, of the epistemic experience; or, in the specific example of the disciplinary society, an echo can be identified as the automated functions of the self.

Inside the Panopticon subjectivity is induced through several paradoxical effects. Trapped among hundreds if not thousands, the occupant of the cell is alone, holding the same position and same relationship to the centre as every other inmate. Despite the emphasis on individuality, there is in fact an equality of fate. The cell is a technology of space that makes one occupant indistinguishable from all others. The panoptic self is the anonymous individual – the self who is oddly not a self but a site of permission for the (mass) productivity of panoptic technology.

Behind the cell, the world-light breaks through grates of iron and passes on namelessly to the tower. The world-light fully exposes the interior of the cell as its waves stretch to the tower. Indeed, the world-light itself is trained by the architecture; it is itself a technology that forces the occupant to experience the tower as illumination. From the cell, the tower is the most prominent feature, surpassing the view of other inmates with whom one shares isolation and surveillance. The exterior world is also forbidden. The enclosed relationship is primary, for it is by controlling space and training vision that the gaze of the subject is to pivot and fall back upon itself. Here again lies a paradox. The Panopticon is totally self-referential; it constitutes the truth that it creates. Inside the Panopticon, the experience of the self and the production of the self have become the same event.

Strangely, the most prominent structure in the Panopticon is hidden. There is no secret in the Panopticon except the interior of the tower. Then, as if to augment even this irony, comes the *pièce de résistance*: this secret is returned to the inmate as exposure. The tower is always present as the point from which the gaze is returned; therefore it is always the exposure of the self to the self. Yet, as the holder of an unverifiable eye, the tower's presence consists of its absence. It is there as the unverifiable; it is in its absence that it is most strongly present as an induced subjectivity. The most obvious expression of power in the Panopticon is omnipresent in effect but impotent in fact – and yet by way of secrecy all the more potent.

Among the manifold ways by which the Panopticon is a series of paradoxical effects, one remains particularly salient. Lines of vision go out from the cell to the central tower and are reflected backward upon the self. This is the echo of self-surveillance that becomes the presupposition of the disciplinary archive. But these lines of vision that echo back and that constitute the possibility of the subject are complicated because they are passive in accordance with the passive nature of visibles as a whole. Thus, the "echo" acts only tacitly to repeat what has already been accomplished at the level of the statement-event. The echo at the level of vision is the repetition of what is accomplished in the statement. The echo in this way *impresses* a sense of necessity into the function of the archive. Though it is tempting to dismiss this so-called "echo" somewhat casually, in fact it constitutes the manner in which the activity of an archive becomes the experience of necessity. An archive's permission is coupled with repetition and necessity. Here then lies the heart of the matter. How can repetition be linked to the experience of necessity in an archive such that the "present" of an archive can be understood as an architecture of knowledge?

PERMISSION AS THE EXPERIENCE OF NECESSITY

Necessity can be a misleading term since its use can imply several meanings. In a philosophical context it can be a simple matter of logic where a conclusion necessarily follows from a premise or set of premises. In metaphysical studies such as theology necessity might identify an ethical foundation on which to construct human activity. But here the meaning is genealogical. The reference is not to an impelling conclusion or an ethical foundation but to the productive effects of archival forces or, as I am saying, the archive permission. Here necessity is to be understood not as a thing (*nomos*) but as a manufactured experience (*episteme*). I call this experience credibility, and I mean the archive environment in which forces produce forms of epistemic persuasion.

The Panopticon again is exemplary for this question. From the tower, the gaze must be, above all, an expert gaze, a standard of normal judgment exercised in the archive space. If the expert's line of vision is not linked to normalcy – if one does not "see things right" – the disciplinary intention of the Panopticon, in this sense, backfires: in place of the trained observer there is a social delinquent. Equally, if the subject of examination does not repeat in the echo the expected standard the gaze casts upon it, the subject is likewise branded delinquent. Delinquency then is a constant threat at the edge of normalcy; it is the "un-thought" of the disciplinary system, the "nothingness" that is incomprehensible to the disciplinary purposes. What holds delinquency at bay is the repetition of normalcy. Insofar as the panoptic structure can repeat its accomplishment, that is, insofar as it can consistently reproduce the network of its statements and hold in its "present" its system of epistemological experience, it can maintain a standard naming of the normal and labelling of the delinquent.

But the activity of repetition (of maintaining or holding present the epistemic experience) is one of tautology. The system produces the sense of normalcy by producing the conditions that create the credibility of the normal statement and that justify the branding of delinquency: the system itself thereby forever engages the self-perpetuating activity of mythmaking. It does so "necessarily" in order to be present – in order to manufacture the conditions of credibility. The archive must "believe" itself. The archive must produce a normalizing standard and then justify itself by means of assuming its standard in its normalizing gaze. In the Panopticon the necessity to label the delinquent or to train the individual or to find the nature of the criminal reflects its systematic tautology. What is seen is what is produced. What is reasoned rests upon what is accomplished in the productivity of statement-events. In this sense necessity, genealogically understood, is always the expressed persuasion of the archive accomplishment.

Necessity is forged in the productivity of statements that bear the constitution of reasoning in an archive. If the archive is to avoid annihilation by way of collapse, the relationships of forces must produce the credibility of repetition; they must produce necessity as a type of momentum set against reversals. Necessity of course is not a choice; individuals within archives do not decide upon it. Again, the intention must be understood genealogically: it is the "effect" of the archive function. It is the experience of the present. It is the reading of space produced in the relationship of forces.

When operating ideally, the Panopticon produces forces to infiltrate the subject and promote the epistemological necessity of subjectivity. The Panopticon becomes the structural reading of the world.[11] Unlike the Middle Ages, where social exclusion is ontologically based (according to the binary pattern of clean and unclean), in the panoptic system binary divisions are dispersed across the whole network. There is no singular, categorical social division but a technology of divisions expressed in any number of ways that work to include and exclude at different levels and across innumerable (yet cellular) spaces. To Foucault modern disciplines multiply the forms of exclusion; disciplines bring the standardizing gaze down to the most local intensity. As Foucault shows, the Panopticon makes a plague victim

11 Foucault, *Discipline and Punish*, 201.

(who is secluded) out of the leper (who is excluded).[12] The Panopticon creates "the tactics of individualizing disciplines [that] are imposed on the excluded;"[13] it produces sets of exclusion by which individuals are classified: normal or abnormal, sane or mad, harmless or dangerous, depressed or manic. The Panopticon functions to reduce space by isolating the "case study" through the constant exposure of the subject to measurements of discipline. "Hence, the major effect of the Panopticon: to induce in the inmate a state of conscious and permanent visibility that assures the automatic functioning of power."[14]

Archival necessity is bound to repetition that plays out in the automatic functions of power. In the Panopticon necessity emerges as a particular form of persuasion generated in the need to satisfy the normalizing gaze of its statements. The Panopticon produces spaces of permission that are credible insofar as they are conforming to (repeating) certain standards of behaviour and certain dictates of truth. This is why Foucault will tell us that such spaces of permission, as I have named them, manifest power as induced pleasures, formations of knowledge, and produced discourses.[15] These spaces of the archive are constrictions, "micro economies" as Foucault might prefer to say,[16] where repetitions are performed. If an archive collapses, then it can be said that *repetition* no longer occurs. The sustainability of an archive lies in its capacity to repeat a particular order of knowledge permitted by a relationship of forces that manufacture its presence as necessity.

It can be understood, then, that repetition relies on two functions: first, eliminating the radical outside; second, creating a fictive "outside" woven from the fabric of the archive interior. For simplicity, let us understand the radical outside as the other and the fictional outside as the manufactured. In the Panopticon, the radical outside is the world beyond the prison, the other that can never be constituted. But the space of the cell nevertheless remains one of productivity; it contrives or fictionalizes a second outside achieved in its orientation toward the normalizing gaze. Caught in the panoptic function, the

12 Ibid.
13 Ibid.
14 Foucault, *Power/Knowledge*, 119.
15 Foucault, *Discipline and Punish*, 181.
16 Ibid., 255.

victim is persuaded to reckon the tower as the outside standard against which deviancy is measured. Even more stealthily, the victim is to accept from this fictional outside the challenge (reflected back) to overcome the deviancy of the self. The panoptic architecture itself creates a permanent *dialectic of interpretation* between the gaze and the cell. A radical appeal to the outside (that is, to what is not prefabricated in repetition) is no longer possible: instead, the experience of the outside is restricted to the terms of the fictional text. In panopticism, the manifest standard of the gaze is the statement that permits the negative measurement of deviancy and thus produces the credible reading of training. Training is necessarily posited against deviancy; deviancy is the necessary reading induced from the outside against which training is the antidote. Foucault is quick to point out this cycle of repetition when he claims that deviancy as the product of the panoptic society complements the proliferation of investigating experts.[17] Still, Foucault's conclusion is too hesitant. It is not enough to describe deviancy as the panoptic *enfant terrible*. It must also stand as the necessary panoptic fiction. Deviancy is the proof for the need of specific forms of knowledge. It goes hand in hand with producing certain forms of knowledge as desire. The panoptic machinery creates deviancy as a type of surreptitious value in order to heighten the experienced necessity of a self-imposed project of the self. This project of the self – this trained self – is panoptic subjectivity. It is repetition that knows many forms: the observance of self-induced boundaries, the restriction to cells of discipline, and the unspoken adherence to (fictionally conceived) self-evident standards.

Foucault concludes the Panopticon analogy by asking, "Is it surprising that the cellular prison, with its regular chronologies, forced labour, its authorities of surveillance and registration, its experts in normality, who continue and multiply the functions of the judge, should have become the modern instrument of penalty? Is it surprising that prisons resemble factories, schools, barracks, hospitals, which all resemble prisons?"[17]

Archival forces circulate through statements to constrict space, create interior experiences of necessity, posit outside points of deviation, and construct regimes of truth that read deviation against normalcy. The question now is how does this fictional activity of power project itself on the social horizon?

17 Ibid., 229.

7

Social Teleology: Archive Tautologies and Theological Difficulties

FOUCAULT'S STUDIES CLEARLY INVOLVE understanding discursive formations as the product of power and as the expression of relationships of power. Furthermore, the lofty idea of teleology, a trans-historical theme that signifies an intention or aim to history, contradicts Foucault's commitment to the mundane, to the local, that he claimed "no teleology would reduce in advance."[1] Therefore, an objection to the introduction of teleology is certainly on the mark.

It must be made clear at the outset that the notion of teleology, along with the qualification that it is "social" teleology, does not summon traditional ideas of transcendence. Social teleology does not seek to name the identity or nature of trans-historical themes hidden yet inherent in world events. The point, rather, is to open discussion about a fictional, even accidental, by-product involved with experience in an archive. This product is an "effect" of the relationships of power in the archive that can be identified as the ineluctable concomitant of the statement-event. For now, emphasis falls on defining social teleology as an event without roots in substructures or superstructures; rather it projects itself from the surface of discourse much like a partner of the forms of discourse within particular systems of production. Indeed, social teleology in the hands of an archivist reverses the transcendental tradition. It is not the veiled essence of present events, and it is not used to expose the "pre-hensive" momentum of general history.[2] It is rather set forward after the event and consequentially related to power. Social teleology is an effect of power

---

1 Foucault, *The Archaeology of Knowledge*, 203.
2 The term "prehension" is from Whitehead, *Process and Reality*.

that arises when power and knowledge are united; its identification is important when considering how certain power/knowledge formations become, in a given archive, desirable statement-events.

SOCIAL TELEOLOGY
AS THE PRODUCTION OF OVERCOMING

Although Foucault does not use the concept of social teleology, it has a basis in his thought. When Foucault raised the spectre of "colonization" and talked about the "penetration" of new practices into older archival forms, he identified how the productivity of one archive order can set the agenda *epistemologically* for another. Minute practices, perhaps even casually regarded, from one era can emerge as major points of orientation in another. "What was an islet, a privileged space, a circumstantial measure, or a singular model, became a general formula."[3] *Discipline and Punish* describes several practices that seem isolated in a previous archive but that become significant in a new setting: the fetishist focus on the body posture of school children, the training of professional soldiers who must demonstrate obedience by the detailed observances of command, and the workshop timetables that create through the repetition of labour a defined social lifecycle.[4] Each case describes late eighteenth-century practices that move, as it were, to the middle of the new panoptic or disciplinary archive. Colonialism, in these instances, is not about political subjugation, though it can involve that, but about the infiltration of precedent practices that redefine linkages in the order of statements.

On the whole, therefore, one can speak of the formation of a disciplinary society in this movement that stretches from the enclosed disciplines, a sort of social "quarantine," to the indefinitely generalizable mechanism of "panopticism." Not because the disciplinary modality of power has replaced all the others; but because it has *infiltrated* the others, sometimes undermining them, but serving as an intermediary between them, linking them together, extending them and above all making it possible

3 Foucault, *Discipline and Punish*, 209.
4 These examples can be found in the notion of "docile bodies." Foucault, *Discipline and Punish*, 135ff.

to bring the effects of power to the most minute and distant elements [italics added].[5]

To the extent that by infiltration Foucault intends a type of colonial substitution of one epistemic order by another, there is merit in comparing his meaning to Antonio Gramsci's concept of hegemony. To Gramsci hegemony is the negative act of one social class containing, controlling, or manipulating another, but it is also and more importantly a positive, revolutionary act of the proletariat. Hegemony involves the ideological persuasion of a system of government, and for this to be successful and lasting it must be desired by the people. Gramsci thought that labour unions ought equally to practice hegemonic acts if a post-revolutionary proletariat order was to last beyond the early generations.[6] In other words, the new order must be the constantly desired order. Similarly, Foucault will employ colonization as if he means hegemonic persuasion. When explaining how the panoptic archive invaded the juridical archive, Foucault presents how a new order of reasoning can persuade older mechanisms to adapt a different configuration of power. Panoptic disciplines "become attached to some of the great essential functions: factory production, the transmission of knowledge, the diffusion of aptitudes and skills, the war-machine."[7] That the Panopticon happens to be in fact a revolutionary design for houses of confinement is hardly Foucault's concern. The Panopticon is not an example of a redesigned prison but of "re-seeing" confinement on the foundations of a newly established epistemology.

Like Gramsci's idea of hegemony, Foucault's colonization has both positive and negative aspects: the negative aspects of the Panopticon are obvious in its pronounced restrictions: the body is confined and isolated; points of reference are limited and controlled within cellular locations. Yet the converse is completely true: the panoptic practice of confining also produces specific openings to a new order of statements, in this case the panoptic system of reason. The disciplinary strategies of the Panopticon ensure the repetition of acts, which we have seen includes the dialectical relation of tower and cell

5 Ibid., 216.
6 See Adamson, *Hegemony and Revolution*, 170–8.
7 Foucault, *Discipline and Punish*, 211

that produces the effect of subjectivity. At the moment when the Panopticon replaced the jury, colonialism occurred in the re-setting of the conditions of the repetition of statement-events. Put succinctly, it can be said that the "successful" supersession of one archive over another involves the infiltration and reorientation of a given pattern of repetition. To Foucault, discipline accomplished this by turning confinement from classical exclusion to modern subjectivity. By means of displacement the new power regime created its own reading of the world.

In the Panopticon the judge of the judiciary archive comes to be seated in the inspector's box of the tower, but the eye of this new formation is all-seeing. In the courtroom as much as the workplace, the hospital as much as the schoolroom, panopticism is the privatization of authority. The foreman, the teacher, the expert, and even co-workers or colleagues cast a trained gaze from one onto another. The effect is sovereignty broken into a million pieces and cast broadly across what Foucault called "a society of normalisation."[8] Foucault did not invoke, but could have, contemporary images of hidden cameras, radar, and thermal imaging. He could have expanded his meaning in more practical ways that might help his reader. That he didn't does not detract from his point: the Panopticon is a device of democracy. Inspection falls on everyone and everyone becomes an inspector not as the masses but as the subject. Inspection is even ingested, creating out of the subject a self-inspecting machine of disciplinary repetition. In the Panopticon every cell occasions the privatization of social norms. This new normal is ancient royal sovereignty turned inside out.

With the general notion of colonial infiltration comes the idea of social teleology. Colonialism involves encountering the "outside" as a frontier of conquest, as a location to be enlightened or trained by the standards of an inside order. Though much has been made of Foucault's relative silence on the issue of colonialism,[9] the basic movement of colonial practice needs to be seen in the archival irony highlighted earlier. The colonial frontier is the fictive product expressing the reading of the world consequentially related to power. Thus, what was previously called the fictive outside now comes home

8 Foucault, *Power/Knowledge*, 107.
9 Stoler, *Race and the Education of Desire*.

to roost: an archive creates the outside from its operations and then projects this fiction categorically forward as a necessary site of over-coming. Since this *necessary project* is created dynamically from power relationships definitive of the archive *episteme* it is called social teleol-ogy; the forged product involves the active network of statement-events and that very network sustains itself as necessity in repetition. This ironic act is the fundamental way in which an archive impresses teleology on its events as if a sideshow mingled with its operation.

In panopticism, the undisciplined subject (the confined) must be persuaded to recognize her or himself as the frontier of overcoming; that is, the subject is a site of disciplinary infiltration. Thus, when one sees how the very elements of a new colonial order come to be through the infiltration of the previously normal reading of the world, one has encountered the manner in which an archive is its own *sui generis*. The archive produces the seeing of the world on the foundations of its own presuppositions formed in its own productiv-ity. Social teleology is an appropriate term for this activity because the activity rests on nothing but the fictional framing of the present as the necessary end (*telos*) of colonial infiltration.

Social teleology, then, begins with the identification of the ar-chive as a condition of tautology. The products of an archive (its forms of knowledge) are consequential of its own practices of rep-etition. Foucault had to conclude that here is where the historian too is always in the catch of history. There is no outside to the ar-chive within which one stands since the seeing of the outside is the product of the inside. Even the question about the outside is al-ready formed from the permission of archive productivity. The practical condition of this tautology is displayed through the Panopticon, which stands as the finale of the whole disciplinary an-alysis. Delinquency, i.e., the abnormal, is the *sine qua non* opposition of the disciplinary society. Yet delinquency itself justifies the disci-plinary society and is even the proof for the necessity of its norms, functions, and systematic training. Foucault exemplifies this when he ties social delinquency to the birth of the prison: the prison cre-ates a social "counter-space" where delinquency is not only the product of the reading of discipline but also the activity against which discipline is necessary. "This delinquency with its specificity is a result of the system; but it also becomes a part and an instrument of it. So that one should speak of an ensemble whose three terms

(police-prison-delinquency) support one another and form a circuit that is never interrupted."[10]

Delinquency is the necessary complement to the long-term perseverance of the panoptic accomplishment. Delinquency justifies the
functioning of panopticism since it continually feeds the need for it.
Though the product of panopticism, delinquency is also its raison
d'être. Out of its functions, the Panopticon creates the norms of subjectivity and casts the corruption of these norms to the fictional outside as the project of overcoming. Then, as if to attack from behind,
the act of overcoming involves the employment of the normal panoptic functions. The fictive outside reinforces the productive inside.
Panopticism is posited as the solution to its own production of failure. The circle is unending. The presupposition is the product. And
the foundation is nothing.

NOTHINGNESS AS TELEOLOGICAL PERSUASION

Panopticism, aside from its very specific form of normalization, is not
different from other archives. All archives, it can be argued, produce
their own experience of the normal, and every archive holds within its
frame the functions of its statements that actively create the interpretation of the world. The interpretation of the world is the product of
power carving out space through discourse (statement-events and
statement-things). Inasmuch as it suppresses and silences, we have
seen that discourse as a function of power privileges, makes available,
and persuades. Foucault suggests even more boldly that the very order
of words is a construction of power thrown at things as their form,
their limit, and their experience. "It is important to conceive of discourse as a violence that we direct at things ... like a practice we impose
on things; and it is in this practice that discursive events find their principle of regularity" or, as said here, their form of repetition.[11]

In the activities definitive of the Panopticon, the sense of the *normal* interpretation of things surfaces in the consistent linkage between mechanisms and judgments (between disciplinary technologies
and training techniques). Recounting the genealogical emergence
of the Panopticon, Foucault relayed in various examples how the

10 Foucault, *Discipline and Punish*, 282.
11 Foucault, *L'ordre du discours* (translation mine), 55.

judiciary functions of the so-called classical era already held within their practice the potential of the newly emerging disciplinary society. A predecessor archive, though not linked directly to its processor as a cause to an effect, is nevertheless the conditional setting of a new horizon.[12] Above all, and in particular, the juridical era "held" for the emerging panoptic gaze a body classified by judgment. The juridical archive gave to the Panopticon the fact of the body as a specific form of analytical space. In effect, the body was already a form of repetition – already a regulated or "normal" location of interpretation – that limited the potential of the succeeding archive. This is how it can be said that a predecessor archive persuades a successor archive. The predecessor is the historic, a priori limitation of succession.

In Foucault's particular analysis he describes the fate of the body in the classical age. He indicates how the body as an object of a new regard was also a "target" of power – a location of discursive violence that constantly shaped the space of its reality and its expression. The classical manner of examining, isolating, measuring, and classifying

12 One will not find "predecessor" and "processor" archives in Foucault; rather, we find a genealogical relationship between two archival forms, such as the juridical and panoptic forms. My expansion of Foucault's genealogical idea involves what I have called the "hold" that a previous archive, like the juridical, has on the succeeding archive, like panopticism. I have employed "hold" primarily for one reason. An archive is identifiable because it is an order of repetition. An archive does not progress – that is, it does not evolve or aim to improve – into another archive: power is the dynamic that changes an archive, not design. An archive, we could say, seeks stability, which is repetition. We must explain archive change on the platform of repetition. Thus a previous archive, which I call the "predecessor," influences, through the horizon that accompanies the archival form of repetition, the potential forms the instability of power can take. We can call these potential forms of instability "sites," as Foucault does when he indicates that the classification of the juridical body is a site of archival disruption. But since the "hold" of the preceding archive is in this way productive, for it inadvertently opens the forms of the sites of instability, it is not simply preceding. It is rather actively preceding: or, it is what I call a predecessor archive. The predecessor participates in the disruption of itself by means of holding in repetition sites of reversal. In the same manner, a processor archive, the archive that emerges from the previous form of repetition, is not simply the next archive but the product of power instability reformulated in a new order of repetition. That new order has its own form of actively "holding" the instability of power; thus, in its repetition it is a projecting of power rather than simply its functioning. Due to this element of projecting I chose to match the term "predecessor" with the term "processor"; an archive processes or projects its horizon as openings for disruption. Thus a predecessor archive has been reformulated into a processor archive.

placed the body within the horizon of a disciplinary technology that would soon be both the vista from which the body is judged and the forum in which the body is trained. Though there is no hand of providence guiding this transition, it must be said that an archive does not emerge haphazardly. The predecessor "holds" the reading of its processor to a conditioned horizon. Even in the case of chance when something new seems to happen out of the blue, that extraordinary event can only happen due to the position already permitted the observer in an archive. The predecessor archive produces the threshold of statement events and orders of knowledge that can be credible as new forms of articulation and practices of power. When this simple point is broken down further such that one seeks to understand how newly manufactured locations or particular types of repetition become desirable, then one is engaged in asking how a new "normalcy" has emerged in the archive and gained a widespread sense of *necessity* for the *proper* reading of the world. In other words, one is beginning to define the question of socially produced teleology.

The question involves understanding how a predecessor archive in its functions will cast its shadow on emerging (processor) events. By shadow I mean the precedent "hold" on the potential of the new order of events. Perhaps it can be said that the shadow is the memory of a former archive now eclipsed. It is as if the weight of an earlier time still drags on the new order of being in the world. Though posed simply, this notion includes two difficulties. One is proving, if possible, that the predecessor shadow of an archive accounts for the epistemological experience of *necessity* in any given system of reasoning; and the second is demonstrating that this archival shadow, on a philosophical level, accounts for the (mis-taken) impression of a categorical a priori.[13] These two points are crucial to understanding an

---

13 "A priori" means prior to experience. There is a longstanding argument, rooted in Kantian metaphysics but certainly emerging from scholastic philosophy, that human beings must assume certain truths in order to experience the stable interpretation of phenomena. Because these truths must be assumed, they are "categorical" or tacit in nature. Space and time are included because it is not possible to experience anything without space (location) and time (duration), and both must be assumed in the act of saying anything about either. From this basic philosophical level one can expand the problem to address a historical a priori and even a religious a priori (as Friedrich Schleiermacher most famously did). The historical a priori appears in Foucault, as we have seen, in his view that statements produce space. Thus, the

archivist's view of history and to articulating new directions for the philosophical contemplation of theology and even the general question of religious experience.

So far, we have seen that a precedent archive will hold the potential of a new order of knowledge to limited possibilities even though it will not define those possibilities explicitly. The example has been Foucault's disciplinary archive emerging from the precedent juridical archive. A new archive, of course, has its own operating space apart from the precedent archive and equally tempers, in its unique practices, openings on its horizon. But the precedent "hold" of the former archive, though no longer the historic present, influences the new order. To the new order it is a shadow that can be called persuasion. Even after its collapse, the precedent is the fact of the space a successor archive has overcome; and, because the precedent is therefore the space of the memory of overcoming, the precedent remains peculiarly at hand in relation to the direction in which the successor archive moves. Keep in mind that the precedent is now the "space of the memory of overcoming" in the *present* archive order: thus, it is the *present* space of *memory*. In relation to the processor archive, the predecessor archive's presence is its absence: its presence is its history – as a location of emergence that disappeared in the fact of emergence. Its "there" is the necessary absence in the actually emerged. So, the precedent is influential by means of being overcome; it is at-hand by

---

product of the statement must be assumed in the experience of the statement as an event: that is, one cannot experience space except as an "order of space" already produced in the statement. In Heidegger, the historical a priori is less difficult. Being in history (historicity) is the presupposition of existence: history is pregiven to the existent's existing. For Heidegger the historical is not a choice but simply what we have fallen into. Schleiermacher argued for a religious a priori by seeking to demonstrate that human existence assumes a relationship to a reality greater than itself. Existence presumes an experience of dependence on another for the being of the self, and Schleiermacher called this the "experience of absolute dependence." Schleiermacher defined this argument in religious terms, claiming that a human being must assume, if even unconsciously, the existence of God. My discussion holds that the a priori experience is an effect of a relationship to a precedent archive. However, there is a slight complication in the sense that while the explanation suggests that the relationship to the precedent is unavoidable, the precedent is not actually there anymore. It is as a ghost, which renders the a priori relationship to the precedent an experience without a foundation. The a priori in my presentation, then, is highly paradoxical: it is both present and absent, necessary yet non-existent. Its appearance is precisely its disappearance.

means of receding. Due to its persuasion being its absence, it is possible to say that the precedent archive haunts the activity of a new archive as if its shadow.

If the functions and productivities of a successor archive continually re-enforce the absence of the precedent archive, then the precedent is a strangely active absence that creates a condition of credibility for acts in the new order. The panoptic body, as an example, continually assumes the classification of the body as a site of reading. Though that act of classification in fact is absent to the panoptic analysis, it nevertheless is that which positioned the body for the Panopticon and accounts for the panoptic assumption of the juridical expression of power. Classification is the memory of the Panopticon and its presupposition even though the principal reasoning of panopticism is not classification but isolation and training. In *Discipline and Punish*, the classical question of the "nature of man" becomes in panopticism the training of gestures.

This anonymous, persuasive hold of absence, as a ghost or a memory or a shadow, nevertheless remains co-present in the active *episteme*. At the level of phenomenology this shadow is an a priori experience. In other words, it is precisely the specific conditions of history, which the image of an archive describes, that explain why the archive function will turn back on itself, back to the permission of its precedent as an a priori grounding, to find the *necessary* sense of its present. But it is of course an appeal to a ghost – to a nothing left as a trace, as Derrida would say, in the current production of memory. Since the relationship to the precedent is in fact a relationship to absence, the force of that relationship lies not in an event but rather in a location of credibility that an event fulfills. The body in panopticism is the event of subjectivity. The credibility of subjectivity lies in the shadow left to the Panopticon of the juridical body whose classification created the horizon of seclusion and training. The body is therefore the space of permission from the old archive that the new panoptic order infiltrates to re-cast as a site of desire, that is, as the credibility of a new power/knowledge formation. The shadow of the precedent archive frames the experience of necessity for the new archive; the former influences the potential of the latter. Precedent archives permit emerging relationships of power that persuade a new recognition and account for the sense of necessary readings that philosophy has traditionally understood as a categorical a priori. Effectively, in the archivist understanding, there is no categorical a priori except as an impression of power and a consequence of location. An a priori is the side effect of the whole archive performance, which, in its play, holds as a concomitant event a social teleological impression. That a new archive seems inevitable from within the experience of its present, that it came into being impressing the moment as the natural development of history, merely reflects the persuasion of the precedent circulation of power that positioned the permission of the new emergence. Permission identifies no categorical a priori (either of perception or of history) but more modestly a side effect of the fact of history as necessarily being archival and necessarily being the product of forces. Again, this whole activity – this anonymous succession of archives that impresses necessity on new or emergent formations – can take the collective name of social teleology and can be understood as the ineluctable effect of archival succession.

In traditional theology, an a priori is invoked to portray the basic mystery of life and the necessary ideal of God as the absolute transcendental. Friedrich Schleiermacher achieved this breakthrough at the birth of modern theology when he coined the expression *Abhängigkeitsgefühl* (feeling of absolute dependence).[14] This same insight remained a key feature of later systematic theology, particularly with Paul Tillich, and continues significantly in the various forms of postmodern religious thought. In brief, the argument rests on Kant's contention that human perception reaches a finite limit, which, accordingly, implies a need to ground experience on something absolute and necessarily outside human limitations, a *mysterion*. Though not named any more explicitly than the noumenal, Kantian inspired religious thought established a relationship to the noumenal on the basis of a leap of faith (to borrow Kierkegaard's famous phrase) and conceived the relationship positively as the ground for a moral imperative. In postmodern philosophical theology the question is not one of a moral imperative so much as the usefulness of the noumenal when contemplating the sense and significance of the concept of God.

The character of the postmodern is rightly described as a turn to linguistics in philosophy. This turn is away from the modern sense of the nature or identity of things to the linguistic and cultural construction of meaning. Foucault's uniqueness lay in his ability to offer the

14 Schleiermacher, *Der christliche Glaube.*

images of an archive, power relationships, and productions of meaning as an alternative to the modern quest for the interior substance or the foundation of things. Essentially, the surface displaces the depth. In the realm of theological speculation, the linguistic turn identifies the limits of language in relation to matters that lie outside language. Jean Luc Marion, for example, speaks of the infinite beyond the constructions (idols) of language;[15] and Charles Winquist speaks of the liminal experience available at the interstices of language (games).[16] But not all postmodern theological expression points to a beyond or outside of language that language itself hides and leave unknowable. Mark C. Taylor celebrates the idea of nothingness, indicating that in fact the very surface of language is actually a new type of profundity. To him, that there is nothing beyond (that is, no substantive referent to linguistic functions but rather only trans-referential functions) is the discovery of a nothingness that changes the mundane from repetition to celebration. "This nothingness transforms the ordinary into the extraordinary," Taylor claims.[17] Similarly, Don Cupitt holds that there is no outside to language, and thus no transcendental foundation to human experience. At best, for Cupitt, religious language can express the art of life and it can, in a constructive fashion, help human beings be human (that is, be their own creation).

I do not intend to follow up these general comments about postmodern theology in detail since my concern is limited to exploring Foucauldian thought and the question of philosophical theology. Foucault's archives offer a very different style of investigation through his displays of linguistic operations, ideas of repetition, and expressions of power emerging in and with statement-events. If these dynamics displace the traditional centre of a priori reasoning in theology, then the idea of God and its historic forms can be tied to the impression of the condition of an archive's existence: to its sense of necessity, to its a priori shadow, and to the "system of its functioning."[18] This is distinct from postmodern theology and the linguistic turn.

15 Marion, *God Without Being.*
16 Winquist, "Theology, Deconstruction, and Ritual Process."
17 Taylor, *About Religion*, 261.
18 Foucault, *Archaeology of Knowledge*, 129.

Presenting these new notions with clarity involves many hermeneutical riddles that the archive analysis invokes. The archive can pre-
clude its own analysis, or at least that of the person who conducts the
analysis, because "it is not possible to describe our own archive, since
it is from within these rules that we speak."[19] But this conundrum
does not prevent the use of the archive analysis as a vehicle to understanding the presence of the concept of God in human history, nor
does it prevent the exploration of theology along rather novel lines
of inquiry.

19 Ibid., 130.

8

The Archive and Theology

THERE ARE FEW PRECEDENTS for philosophically "thinking" the concept of God in the archivist way: employing articulables and visibles, permissions and resolutions, and shadows and side effects. It is a struggle to take these terms, which are not even commonly employed in the study of Foucault, from their setting in the archive to the context of philosophical theology. First, the archivist question is not the same as traditional questions in the philosophical contemplation of theology. In the latter, questions generally concern the compatibility of the idea of God with the limits of reason. This is essentially an apologetic task: it is an effort to find a place for God either as the mysterious *other* outside reason or via a functional *language game* within the operations of reason.[1] Meanwhile, the archivist question is not apologetic but more directly an inquiry into the production of the concept of God. It is a question of how "God" is credible, that is, epistemically permissible.

Theological investigations that do incorporate Foucauldian analysis tend to settle for revising the concept of God for the purposes of religious studies.[2] But the archivist must bracket the notion of a revision

---

1 I refer the reader back to the introduction where I recounted the tracks of philosophical theology like rivers in the flow of the Western tradition. There, the attempt was to distinguish between the hermeneutical contemplation of the concept of God (here the mysterious other) and the social scientific concept of God (here a language game).

2 Among the scholars who have most forthrightly taken Foucault into religion studies, Carrette, Bernauer, and Flynn have successfully questioned the way Foucault's thinking has challenged and changed religious thought. However, the direct affirmation that the God concept is a fictional by-product of the archive is far from their analysis. Only Don Cupitt approaches this question, but by a different route.

entirely. The present question is not how best to articulate the concept of God or how best to employ God in philosophical analysis. Neither is it a question of determining the usefulness of an ineffable and incomprehensible other that can still serve the task of establishing a liminal relation to all that is.[3] Rather "God" is a product of the archive, a product of its statements and its relationships of force, and the question is how an archive produces the credibility of this metaphysical space.

The present subject, then, is the philosophical investigation of the concept of God as an event in the archive, and the problem is one of explaining how an archive can impress or persuade credibility for metaphysical statements through the function and flow of its events. The question brings back the basic archive elements: light and language, power and limits, horizons and permissions. Since this unique style of questioning relies on what has been accomplished prior, a review of the language used and conclusions drawn so far will help set up the questions to be explored.

THE QUESTION FOR THEOLOGY IN AN ARCHIVE

In the earliest parts of this investigation, the term "constriction of possibility" was shown to be crucial for comprehending how an archive functions. The term intends not only to describe the conditional setting in which an event is manifest in an archive but also to affirm that an event is always produced locally as an emergent point – as the present or the moment – within the active matrix. This setting is a "constriction" primarily because it is "there" (open to the gaze) through the specific limitations of architectures and technologies, language and light that produce it.

Equally, the constriction permits to the immediate situation a potential horizon. Though it can be said in very broad terms that history is arbitrary and that archive events are merely constrictions in possible activity, the point nevertheless is absolutely not that archive events as locations emerge haphazardly. Constriction is an essential term because it identifies how the potential of the horizon is qualified. The constriction of possibility is double-edged: it identifies the location of an event and it describes how archival forces permit (limit) a spectrum of potentiality for successive events at specific

3 Winquist, "Theology, Deconstruction, and Ritual Process."

locations. The term, then, holds within it the distinction between the event (constriction) and the horizon of the event (potential).

The general understanding of an archive and its events as a series of constricted possibilities raised the question of exactly how an event emerges within archival conditions. The answer aligned several elements that involve the notion of an archive occupation. The archive occupation first describes the limits of an archive space, that is, the expanse of its circulation of discourse or its epistemic reach; then, it describes how these spatial limits produce forms of archival permission. Here the main insight is that an occupation of space is always prior to the employment of space. The statement form is always prior to the reasoning (epistemic) form. Therefore, beyond the need to describe an epistemic structure – beyond the need to address architectural types or scientific paradigms – there lies the need to examine the role of light and language (these being the building blocks of both the present constriction of visibles and articulables and the generators of the permissible horizon) by which an archive occupation occurs. In the end, examining archive functions brings into question the elements of language and light in order to account for the space of permission in which these functions perform.

Language-being, which in Foucault is the primary expression of the statement, was given as the active means by which the boundaries of an archive are drawn; the statement was given as a practice that is before (a priori in relation to) the visible and, as language-being, active and infinite in relation to the visible. Statement-events both as discourse (language) and material (architecture) emerge as markers of space, opening an archive to forms of occupation. Statement-events can also alter an archive or, from the fringe, enter the centre of an archive to recast it. The shift from the juridical archive to panopticism was presented as one such case, but Foucault gives many examples as he recounts shifted epistemic orders between the seventeenth and nineteenth century.

Visibles, on the other hand, are not emergent in the same sense as statements. Visibles are passive in that the "seeing" of space is according to the occupation already established in the statement-event. One cannot see what is not stated. But again, the structuring of the stated is no automatic or isolated event. It remains a constriction of possibility in that it represents the productivity of multiple and mutual relationships of power that circulate in, define, and produce the archive.

The consideration of the statement led inevitably to the consideration of power. This is also true in the development of Foucault's
thought; with Foucault the statement, in the end, is power. The statement is always in a place (or is always a location) in relation to other
statements, and may be privileged, ignored, or scorned depending
on the operating epistemic order, its location in that order, the reverberations of its emergence, and whatever competition it may engage.
The statement is constantly a position; it is inevitably in tensive relation or battle, as Foucault said, with other statements that traverse an
archive and that define its forms. Power and the statement are in-
separable insofar as, whether through material (such as technology)
or articulation (such as teaching), the statement composes the order
of the archive by means of locating events. Even when the event is
such a thing as "madness," the archive remains the presupposed order of epistemic judgment that locates the statement of madness.
The act of locating is in effect the work of power because it is emergence in an interpretive matrix or what I have called the credible
event. The statement and power go together as the productive relationship definitive of an archival form, and in this way Foucault uses
the expression power/knowledge to indicate that the *epistemic* order
of an archive is at the same time the condition of power within it.

Additionally, it was noted that for Foucault power is never really
negative. Certainly, power can prohibit or suppress acts (this, for example, is the dominant characteristic of its juridical forms), and in
this way power can be described negatively. But power is always a flow
of forces in the archive that emerge in forms to create relationships.
In the Panopticon the flow of power creates relationships of discipline and training. So, even though power can inhibit an act or suppress it, it is still "positive" in the sense that negative acts continue to
create the condition of possibility for events. Even negative acts, we
can say, are involved in composing the conditions of credibility. Power
therefore is always positive in the sense that it is always productive. It
both suppresses and makes advantageous certain acts, both creates
and limits the potential of an event, both unites and disperses the association between events, both opens and closes the spaces of an archive. For convenience we can say that power is both negative and
positive, but in effect Foucault's breakthrough involves understanding that both aspects are productive and thereby "positive." Power
cannot inhibit one form of being present in an archive without

producing another form. Power, as Foucault claimed, "needs to be considered as a productive network which runs through the whole social body," much more than as a negative instance whose function is repression.[4]

In order to explain the productivity of power, it was necessary to identify the forms through which power passes, recombines, and distributes itself in an archive. This was done by focusing on the positive effect the relationship of forces has on the location of a specific event. In the particular setting of modernity, relationships are fabricated out of machines and techniques through which power acts to enclose and objectify both the archive agent and the discursive activity. When an individual is "trapped," whether as a prisoner, school child, or patient, the productive consequence of this constriction (i.e., the hold on the potential horizon) given in disciplinary forms is subjectivity: the agent becomes a self-regarding and ultimately self-judging subject. Hence, the Panopticon demonstrates that power, far from being a reductive analysis of culture, poses the very complexity of the archive and problematizes it. Power intimately carves out, in the forms of its circulation, the condition of the archive's constricted possibility. Every event emerges in the constricted setting consequentially since the stating and seeing form is already engrained in the environment of its actuality. This activity of power in relation to the human agent can be understood as the emergence of a *credible* (or recognizable or even desirable) *product* permitted to a local setting. In the relationships of power and their consequent production of permission, the event (for the agent) impresses itself socially as meaningful. An order of credibility is the archive project.

Once the union of the statement and power was expressed, the discussion turned to how an archive comes to occupy a space and how "recognition" occurs within that space. Recognition arises at the local level as the seeing and stating of the archive project. In panopticism, recognition of the project is presented as the resolution of subjectivity before the project of overcoming delinquency.

To expand this analysis dynamically, one can turn to Foucault's idea of infiltration and, additionally, to the concept of social teleology which I introduced. The first describes colonization: the movement of new techniques into and over spaces occupied by others.

4 Foucault, *Power/Knowledge*, 119.

Such a movement includes a type of raison d'être defining the motives of the acts of infiltration. The tower, for example, displaces the jury because it is the technical way to focus resolutely on the body that the juridical archive had held in potential. The second term, social teleology, describes generally how necessity (produced through the forms of the infiltrating order) is concomitant with each emerging event. As the infiltrating order imports a new archive project (*telos*), it brings as a type of side effect the reading of the world that makes the new project desirable. The new project is the system of being in the world necessarily according to the archive project of overcoming. Again, in panopticism, this is the (necessary) resolution of the self-transcending self.

Social teleology implied an archive's "side effects." In particular, while side effects can take many forms – such as teleology – the main point is that a side effect is an expression of the resolution of the archive at a specific location and in a certain way. Side effects should be understood as what is "available" in an archive given its form of production, its arrangements of space, and its activity of statements. Side effects denote the sense of dependence (recognition) and the project reading (anticipation) present with every local event. Hence, the Panopticon was used to show the production of event recognition (the problem of training) and anticipated resolution (the self-transcending self). The reasoning and the justification and the senses of urgency that emerge within forms of recognition and that are resolved in anticipation are called the side effects. These effects condition and aim the archive project as if its concomitant shadows; they create the complex activities of social teleology.

These preliminary considerations now allow the understanding of the concept of God as emerging anonymously as a particular type of metaphysical side effect produced in archival activities. Instead of seeking to defend a God concept or its usefulness historically for comprehending human nature and human endeavours, an archivist analysis of the concept of God will problematize the concept in the various formulations of recognition and resolution within archive events. Indeed, as I will suggest, the concept of God understood as a resolution to archive events is a *normal* metaphysical expression. The normal expression must be set in contrast to the considerations philosophical theology can address when Foucauldian archival analysis is taken seriously.

WHEN GOD IS NORMAL

In claiming that the concept of God is a side effect of the archive activity, what is really being said? Is the point to argue that there is no God? Is it another complicated way of repeating Nietzsche's famous claim that God is dead? The answer is a definite no. The intention is to account for the God concept completely within the productivity of an archive. Whether that concept should be accepted as true or false is not the substance of the debate. The centrepiece is rather the question of how the concept of God can be accounted for as a side effect and what this means to the philosophical contemplation of the idea of God. To this end, the God concept is necessarily linked to emergent events and rests upon archive visibles and articulables.

Admittedly, examining the concept of God in relation to "visibles," as Foucault and Deleuze comprehended them, is a novel and perhaps unusual task. To be clear, it is not a question about a "vision" of revelatory or ecstatic experience; the question rather concerns how a metaphysical perception (such as the God concept) can make "sense" as an event in human experience. Thus, the focus is on *the capacity to perceive a metaphysical event.*

Visibles are passive, and in the Panopticon their passivity consists of being thrown back upon the enclosed subject as the echo of the statement. The visible replicates in display what has already been constructed in the statement. In the Panopticon, the enclosed subject sees the tower and thus "sees" the structure of the statement repeated in lines of vision: vision reproduces the order of the tower and cell in the experience of subjectivity. The tower is a certain kind of material statement, but the relationship to it from the cell is also a visible event repeating the order of the statement composed in the tower and cell relationship. This is the visible's "echo": its repetition of what the statement already is and has already accomplished.

In terms of the capacity to perceive a metaphysical event, the echo of light-being (inscribed in the visible) is highly significant. Even though it has been argued that "light-being" is passive in relation to "language-being," the passive nature of light does not mean it cannot be a positive element in perception. So, even though the visible echoes the accomplishment of the statement, this does not mean that the statement has no dependence on the visible. Rather, the echo is taken as the foundation of a relationship to the horizon. The statement produces the space of the archive, the visible repeats the space of the statement, and the statement then presumes the visible in the act of projecting the horizon of the archive. Accordingly, the visible does play a role, and it is the role of presumption. How can that be?

In the Panopticon it might be thought that the horizon is the tower, for from within the cell the tower lies before the subject as its vision. It is the literal horizon. But there is really another horizon lying in the productivity of panopticism: this is the horizon of the self. The individual in the cell looks upon the tower, but the more important act, the definitive act of the disciplinary society, is the act of the individual looking back upon the self. Indeed, the self is the horizon in panopticism, for the self becomes (on behalf of itself) the eye of the watching tower. The disciplined self is the project, the aim and goal, of this archive. In this sense, the visible element, which here is self-regard, is the foundation of the horizon – for the horizon refers to the project (the projecting forward) of the archive, and in the Panopticon the *projecting forward* is the return of the regard from the tower as the normal aim of the self. The self becomes a tower unto itself. And, Foucault proclaims, "Visibility is a trap."[5] But it is more than this. Visibility is the project of the trap.

The role of the visible can be demonstrated equally well in the juridical experience that preceded panopticism. In the juridical archive the project is classification, and classification comes about by the judgment used to divide space into categories: distinctions among the severity of crimes, criminal traits, and personality disorders. But the statement of classification gives rise to (opens the space for) the visible counterpart, which is the positioning of things. The juridical archive produces the project of placing things in their right order according to their nature, and in *Discipline and Punish* Foucault recounts how in the juridical archive it is a question of aligning a punishment according to the nature of a crime. This of course easily gives rise to the invasion of the disciplinary archive that converts the "position" of things to the "training" of the self. Yet, in the juridical archive the self is of a different order. The self is in an objective position: it is a classified nature, an ordered problem, a social class, a gender, a status, or a professional occupation. The statement of classification is

5 Foucault, *Discipline and Punish*, 200.

repeated in the visible as the nature of the thing. Thus the concern for seeing the nature of a thing becomes the project of the object-making statement.

When one contemplates archival side effects, it is the visible that is more significant because the archive project (such as uncovering the nature of things or idealizing the self) rests upon the ground of perception. Accordingly, even as light-being is passive, it is nevertheless constitutive in terms of metaphysics. Metaphysics, in short, is the active (mis)taking of the echo in light-being as the ground of perception. Yet effectively that ground is fiction: that is, it is merely the replication of what has already been accomplished in the statement; or, in another way, it is a type a side effect of the fact of the statement.

Since, then, metaphysics and the concept of God are *the replication in the visible of what has already been accomplished in the statement,* one can say that God (and indeed metaphysics), while a side effect, is nevertheless a *normal* event. The word normal is used to indicate that what is happening at the level of perception is what is permitted at the level of the archive. The concept of God found in the juridical archive and in the Panopticon is normal. It is normal because it is a product; it is the repetition of the statement that, in the visible, projects itself as perceptual ground.

The apologetic tradition of Christian theological speculation can therefore be called normal theology. The tradition merely seeks to define God at the level of culture, whether that consists of presenting God as Aristotle's unmoved mover, determining God in relation to evolution, or recasting Kant's noumenal world as the divine mystery. Each idea of God is consequential of the activity of the statement producing the visible as the ground of the concept. The God concept is an achievement of an already functioning condition, expressing an already operating teleology, and re-stating an already accomplished side effect. In all these senses, in terms of the archive, the God concept is normal (it is the projected ground of the accomplished).

Naturally, these claims call for an example of what is meant by "normal theology." But one example cannot do all the work required to review the long history of philosophical theology in its apologetic or normal forms. Such an undertaking would require many volumes of historical analysis and is clearly outside the present concern. Instead, the task can be demonstrated more generally through a theme from the Christian tradition. Since the Panopticon has been central to this investigation, we can turn to the complementary tradition of liberal theology that relied specifically on a priori reasoning, which is the side effect of the disciplinary archive. I will look at the theme of sin and salvation (or redemption) as it is found in the work of Paul Tillich, one the outstanding apologetic theologians of the twentieth century.

In the Christian context, the basic division between God and human beings (*imago Dei*) is regarded as either the consequence or the condition of sin,[6] and the working out of this problem concerns grasping and resolving human nature in the hope of salvation. But because "sin" and "salvation," since the Enlightenment, have become foreign words to a scientific understanding of life (and the words themselves are rooted in ancient concepts of human life and culture), the quest of theology in modern times included the translation of traditional concepts for modern sensibilities. Tillich took this challenge most seriously and in the process of developing his systematic theology created a modern language for the comprehension and proclamation of basic ancient notions. "The 'situation' to which theology must respond is the totality of man's [sic] creative self-interpretation in a special period."[7] To Tillich, the "situation" of our particular period was "depth psychology" and the task was to determine a theological language that could address the deeply seated needs of the human psyche. Psychologically, human beings experience a separation from "being" which Tillich called estrangement. He posited estrangement in place of sin as the condition of being in the world. Beings or ontic "things" can be pursued in life as a means of fulfillment, but only union with the ontological ground of Being resolves the situation of estrangement. Tillich could variously call this resolution "courage" and "faith," but in his *Systematic Theology*, he put forward the moving expression "New Being."[8] In this, Tillich is repeating in modern form the famous confession of Augustine: "you have created us for yourself, and our hearts are restless until they find their rest in you."[9]

6 The religious habit today is to interpret "sin" almost strictly personally. Sin in early Christianity was far more structural than personal: it involved living in relation to (and even under) the imperial power of Rome. Nevertheless, my comments are specific to Tillich and to his commentary on modern alienation.

7 Tillich, *Systematic Theology* 1: 4.

8 Tillich, *Systematic Theology* 2.

9 Augustine, *Confessions* (trans. Pine-Coffin), I.1.

We can see in Tillich, with no intention of being condescending and with the full recognition of his major accomplishment, how easily his theology represents a structure of resolution in the social teleological project of his time. His is the theology of the ontic subject who must find reunification with an ontological foundation; it is a theology of panopticism in which there still exists a singular reality, an "is" behind what is, that can be cast as true identity. The question is to aim that identity at, to align it with, the a priori project in which the subject is caught. That a priori ground for Tillich is Being, and thus the project of theology is the resolution of the problem of personal being with the ground of Being or (if stated as panopticism) the reconstitution of the self before the tower as the self-regarding self – the trained self, the self at peace with the project of the self. The apologetic enterprise of theology can be called "normal" because it can take the side effect projects of the archive as the theological task of proclamation. Of course, this does not mean that apologetic theology is incapable of being critical of its cultural or political setting; it does not mean that apologetic theologians cannot be profoundly poignant in comments or analysis. What it does mean is that as a speculative endeavour philosophical theology can easily presume the archive's productivity, getting caught up in its perceptual ground, and even inadvertently defining its spirit. It becomes the "defence" of the operating social teleology. The criticism of philosophical theology from the archivist point of view rests on its failed hermeneutical task, for the apologetic tradition participates in archival productivity without recognizing that its foundation is a side effect and its statements are the project of a specific social teleology.

Insofar as philosophical theology is consequential of the permission of the archive, the concept of God is a side effect produced out of the archive's activity. Such a claim may seem innocent enough; however, one must recognize that it is exactly the opposite of the apologetic tradition. God, even in postmodern theology, is conceived as the mystical *outside* and the *other* who is critically related to human nature. Yet, an archivist understanding denies that an outside exists to any given archive other than as a fictional side effect. The concept of God is created internally in the order of the statement before the concept is permissible as speculation. The God concept emerges from the shadows arising from the forms of perception. Traditionally, philosophical theology simply has presumed the accomplishments of the archive and projected them forward as another form of resolution. Because this whole activity is a performance of permission, it is right to call it a normal archive expression.

AUGUSTINE: THE SELF AS ARCHIVE RESOLUTION

Augustine provides another example of philosophical theology operating within the normal functions of an archive. He worked out the problems of theology in antiquity, yet he marks the threshold of the Middle Ages. His problem is based in ancient philosophical assumptions, but we can see that he places the basic problem of the ancient self, which I will call the problem of the One and the many, on the stand of a new resolution. He is, it can be said, the statement of a new archive.

We need to begin with Augustine's basic understanding of the self and his proposed resolution to the problem of the self, and this means that we need to begin with his understanding of Manichaeism. One could argue whether Manes (whose approximate dates are 216 to 276 CE and whose existence is occasionally debated[10]) and the movement associated with him, Manichaeism, truly espoused a dualism, that is, held that there are two distinct and equally powerful realities, one of the spiritual world and one of the material world. The ancient Manichaean movement, rooted in Zoroastrianism, played with images of light and darkness, principles of good and evil, and viewed the material world as a type of dyadic play between these two forces. Zoroastrianism, nevertheless, remained monotheistic, and Manichaeism shared that same definition. Darkness, in this system of philosophy, is a shadow cast by the principle of light, and human beings must struggle to choose light in a world mixed with shadows. Still, Augustine seems not to have taken it this way.

To Augustine, the Manichaean teaching was an excuse for moral irresponsibility. He could "sin" and blame the act on "something else inside me (I knew not what) but which was not I."[11] Augustine understood darkness as a second and autonomous principle set outside the boundaries of his will and acting as if it were an independent force invading and possessing his members. While this was not Manichaean

10 The problem lies in "Mani" being a title rather than a name and the consequent obfuscation of the founder whose name is unknown and who left no extant records.
11 Augustine, *Confessions*, V.10.18.

teaching, it was nevertheless Augustine's perception of it and it betrayed a fundamental philosophical problem that defined both his concern and that of his age: the problem of the One and the many. This is the problem of determining a principle or singular substance that lies behind the appearances of change, multiplicity, and dissimilarity in the phenomenal world.[12]

In Neo-Platonism the transcendental, unapproachable, and nameless "One" was apperceived in the cosmic order and mimicked existentially in the human condition. Hence the physical world, including the human body, is a type of allegory that betrays a hidden meaning. The human "mind" (*nous*) hints of a universal Mind; the *psyche* is to the body as the *logos* is to the universe; being in existence is belonging to the primal generation (Being) of all that is. In Neo-Platonism, the physical is the allegory of the spiritual, and in the Roman imperial context the question is not to will the good (as in the Manichaean system) so much as to imitate in the flesh the natural superiority of the mind: a demonstration of mastery of the physical appetite by way of the spiritual appetite. In contrast to Neo-Platonism, Augustine believed he had found a better way to represent and solve the problem of the One and the many, and in so doing he created a Christian systematic theology that also served as an ethical and political philosophy. Arguably, his reading of Manichaean philosophy inspired a system where, I hope to show, he could work with two realms battling over the soul.

Notwithstanding the fact that Christianity, especially through Augustine, adopted many Neo-Platonic insights, the problem of the One and the many persisted. It can be understood generally as a problem of imitation.[13] The isolated and a-physical "One" is constantly elusive to the physical conditions of life and its state of ignorance.

12 I have capitalized "One" to indicate that I am talking about the Western idea of substance or essence signifying (by means of participation in) a highest possible being.

13 This is a general term but Foucault illustrates it in several ways in *The History of Sexuality* 2. For example, Foucault refers to Aristotle's idea that children do not always resemble their parents because the minds of their parents were occupied with other thoughts during the act of copulation (124). Thus, there is an approximate relation between child a parent: the child imitates the parent but is separated from the pure identity. In another case, Foucault reminds us of the "principle of isomorphism" (215) where sexual relationships imitate social relationships, but this principle is extensive since social relationships imitate nature, which in turn imitates mind. In other words, antiquity has a hierarchy of imitative relationships generated from the "One" – the elusive but somewhat proximate principle of the universe.

Consequently, a type of metaphysical gap exists between the two orders such that the overcoming of bodily weakness consists of acting out or being in tune with the "a-physical" realm while still remaining in the physical state. The acting out could occur in several forms, but to Foucault its main expression in antiquity is self-mastery; among philosophical schools self-mastery could consist of asceticism, dietary restrictions, or specific practices of discipline. The ancient world attempted, though this is still a general conclusion, to solve the problem of bodily appetites by overcoming them through the individual mind participating in the universal mind: it is a question of imitating the universal mind in the daily practices of life.

Christianity brought to this context a unique ability to alter the practice of imitation by way of its doctrine of incarnation. Although the incarnation then produced a new set of problems in which the Middle Ages engaged (such as Anselm's need to reason why the incarnation was necessary and Occam's belief that it wasn't), the attractiveness of a simple point of synthesis (in Christ) not only drew the attention of the greatest minds of late antiquity but also appealed broadly to the masses. Augustine remains one of the most influential thinkers in Western history.

A brief example of how Augustine changes the ancient question can be drawn from his writing. Augustine articulates a new kind of problem, which is one of confession, that supplants ancient imitation. Though Augustine employs Christian language and concepts, we can note that he shifts the necessary point of mediation to the encounter of history.

> Now as [human beings] were lying under this wrath [of God] by reason of their original sin, made the more heavy and deadly in proportion to the number and magnitude of the actual sins which were added to it [i.e., to the state of original sin], there was need for a Mediator, that is, for a reconciler, who, by the offering of one sacrifice, of which all the sacrifices of the law and the prophets were types, should take away this wrath ... Our being reconciled to God through a Mediator, and receiving the Holy Spirit, so that we who were enemies are made [children] ("For as many as are led by the Spirit of God, they are the [children] of God"[14]): this is the grace of God through our Lord Jesus Christ.[15]

14 Augustine here quotes from Romans 8:14.
15 Augustine, *The Enchiridion on Faith, Hope, and Love*, 41–2.

The ancient problem of imitation, which was constructed with notions of self-mastery, essentially disappears in Augustine as the statement-event of Western antiquity. The project is no longer imitation. The archive resolution is no longer mastery. In Augustine the new project involves a Mediator, before whom the right relationship is the confession of the permanent shortcomings of the human condition. The Augustinian "side effect," if you will, is the general social teleological functioning of a helplessly corrupted soul. It is now the universal mind, in Christ, that decides the fate of the soul.

Augustine manages to make imitation a permanent impossibility so that self-mastery becomes useless because it becomes the privilege of the Mediator alone. The only means to reconcile the self to the archive project is to confess the truth of the Mediator. The Mediator is the new necessary point of overcoming, that is, the new archive project. This project, the archivist insists, is the effect of the statement of a permanent division Augustine called original sin.

Foucault focuses extensively on antiquity only in the second and third volumes of *The History of Sexuality*, where he discusses the aristocratic ideal of self-mastery. While Foucault understood that, from an earlier Greek setting to a later Roman setting, self-mastery shifted from the mastery of pleasure (what he relates to the Greek *aphrodisiac* and *chērsis*[16]) to the mastery of the self as an of act pleasure (which he identities with Seneca's use of *gaudium* and *laititia*[17]), he did not place this in the general philosophical problem of the One and the many. Yet we can understand that the reasoning of pleasure had this very structure as its *episteme*, for pleasure was a question of aligning the body and the soul or of placing the physical experiences of life in metaphorical juxtaposition to the principles of reason. This is why I called the act, generally, imitation. In the third volume of *The History of Sexuality* Foucault states, "The reasonable soul thus has a dual role to play: it needs to assign a regimen for the body that is actually determined by the latter's nature, its tensions, the condition and circumstances in which it finds itself. But it will be able to assign this regimen correctly only provided it has done a good deal of work on itself: eliminated the errors, reduced the imaginings, mastered the desires

16 Foucault, *History of Sexuality* 2: 37.
17 Ibid, 3: 66.

that cause it to misconstrue the sober law of the body."[18] The "nature" that Foucault focuses on in this quotation is the ancient cosmic
order. The body is trained not as in modernity by finding its inner self
but by using itself metaphorically as the còsmos. In short, by re-cast-
ing the self as the stasis of the cosmic, ancients solved the problem of
the One and the many.

In Augustine, Christianity was capable of expressing the body and
soul as a united experience of subjectivity set apart from God but
whose mastery lies in a reconciling act with the divine image (in the
Middle Ages, expressed powerfully in mystical writings). But Augustine
is the generator of this teleological project. Rather than understanding the soul as the guide and reason of the body, Augustine defines an
archive where the problem of the One and the many is converted to
the confession of alienation and the acceptance of reconciliation in
the Christ event. Augustine in many respects set a pattern for Western
thinking by linking self-reconciliation to confession and self-discovery
to the condition of human finitude. That is to say, he addressed the
chief dilemma of his time within the permission of a social teleology
by introducing a Christian resolution that converted to confession the
precessor statement of imitation.

TWO OPTIONS FOR ARCHIVAL THEOLOGY

Augustine, as one of the most influential thinkers in Western history,
is a unique example of how theological speculation emerges as a
resolution within the functions of an archival project. And exactly
due to Augustine's stature, it becomes all the more clear why it is significant in our time not only to understand theological apologetics
but also to re-imagine the meaning and style of theological investigations. An archival investigation of the concept of God as a product
begins where the normal tradition remains silent. It starts with the
examination of statements and side effects, and then it relays the
presence of theology in history not as apologetic insight but as a system of productivity.

Still, the example of Augustine invokes another image inasmuch as
Augustine failed to move beyond the normal functions. The question
is, Can there be another fruitful avenue of study for theology, in light

18 Ibid., 133.

of the archive, besides portraying the form of a God concept and examining its productive effects? Can the question of the normal turn on itself? Indeed, can one investigate the social teleological resolution of an archive in such a way as to stand in a transgressive relationship to it?

The trouble in an archive, of course, is exactly that the undertaking of its criticism belongs to the realm of its permission. It too can be understood as a side effect. The archive affords no "outside" position and no "word" that is not also a location. Still, it does permit the inversion of the location. Essentially, statements can stand outside themselves within themselves. This can be understood as a crack or as interstices within the archive. We have noted with Foucault that such moments can account for reversals of power and alterations in archives. Theology can grasp this and can imagine in deliberate forms a relationship to the moment that is outside itself in the act of being itself. Rather than normative, this act can be called parabolic.

Thus there are two possibilities in an archivist approach to theology. One is a redefinition of systematic theology as the history of systems of God. I will call this archaeological theology. A second possibility is theology as the critical activity of the present. This requires parabolic thinking, and I will call this option genealogical theology. Taken together they can be called archival theology.

9

Archaeological Theology

IN THE SECOND PREFACE to *The Gay Science* (*Die fröhliche Wissenschaft*), Nietzsche tells the reader that the work arose from his newfound strength after one of his long illnesses. "'Gay Science': that signifies the saturnalia of a spirit who has patiently resisted a terrible, long pressure – patiently, severely, coldly, without submitting, but also without hope – and now who is all at once attacked by hope, the hope for health, and the *intoxication* of convalescence."[1]

It is easy to contrast one type of thinking with another as sickness to health, and perhaps overdone. Postmodern thinking, additionally, makes such contrasts difficult; after all, by what set of relationships is one judged sick or well, and where is one standing when such labels are cast? Still, from the archivist standpoint, there is something familiar about persisting "patiently, severely," and even "coldly" with a new perspective. Time with the archive is a type of convalescence: it is a recovering from the tradition of theology by shifting the question to how religion is thought.

The primary shift occurs in the understanding of history and the idea of God. An archivist is not engaged in the history of ideas and does not seek progressive refinements in the idea of God. Archaeology is concerned with the history of the production of God. This is a forthright uncovering of the epistemic layers of theology: the power/knowledge relationships in which the idea of God is conceived, that is, in which the idea is fabricated in a system of social teleological resolution.

Although accounting for the idea of God as a cultural-historic product invokes nineteenth-century atheistic theology – Feuerbach, Strauss,

---

1 Nietzsche, *The Gay Science*, 32.

and Marx – the analysis is not the same. Rarely does a theologian bracket the very question of God, God's existence or non-existence, and God's primal if mythical origin in favour of the phenomenon of the linguistic production of God. Still, many could object that such a claim is too lofty and far from accurate, for there is certainly in our time the question about "how to think God after the death of God."[2]

The objection can be granted, but it still presumes that the presentation of theology is "about" something: about the role of God and God's usefulness even if reduced to a cultural "meme."[3] An archivist approach, on the other hand, is novel because the examination concerns the means of production: the manner in which the event as a location of power produces the desire for the resolute idea. It is never a question about the idea in itself: whether the idea is a thing or a not thing, whether it conveys mythic value or is incapable of such hermeneutical significance. Archival theology is about the moment. It asks why, in the dynamics of an archive, did the event emerge in the field we have called the constriction of possibility?

Properly speaking this is a question of archaeological theology. The God concept is comprehended as a side effect of the linguistic event, but the archaeological explanation seeks to demonstrate that the God concept is a credible side effect, a moment conceivable at the location as resolution. In short, archaeological theology is the examination of the statement in order to investigate the event of God. Along with the Panopticon, a second image that helps to expand and explore archaeological theology comes out of Foucault's reading of Raymond Roussel.

SEEING THEOLOGY IN THE ARCHIVE

In the clever and obscure story *Locus Solus*, Foucault discovered a new world.[4] Roussel's book is the fictional account of a prominent scientist named Martial Canterel who invites some colleagues to his estate. There, he shows off a series of inventions, each stranger and more complex than the previous. In one, fresh corpses have been injected

2 Taylor, *About Religion*, 3.
3 Ibid., 88–101. I refer particularly to Taylor's discussion of Dawkins's *The Extended Phenotype*.
4 Foucault, *Death and the Labyrinth*.

with a fluid called "resurrectine" that causes the bodies to re-enact perpetually the most memorable event of their past lives. Furthermore, the corpses are caged, for the purposes of display, in a huge glass unit. From this Foucault concludes that for Roussel machines do not manufacture beings; they maintain things in their state of being.[5]

In the Panopticon a machine disperses power and produces the event; but with the Roussel example, there is greater emphasis on another familiar but still important aspect. That aspect is repetition, which relates to the basic question of technology. The Panopticon above all is a machine of repetition, and Foucault draws his insight here from Nietzsche, Heidegger, and particularly Deleuze.[6] Technological functions perform repetition as anonymous tasks. To make a technical device work properly every agent who uses it must do so in an identical way. A bank machine does not distinguish between individuals who use it but rather between functions that operate it. The automatic checkout requires everyone to operate the same buttons. Every individual employs technical functions the same way. To a degree unparalleled before the industrial age, in the technical society the individual releases individuality (peculiarity) to anonymity (technology), and as Deleuze says (taking his inspiration from Hume), "repetition changes nothing in the object repeated, but does change something in the mind which contemplates it."[7] In a sense, an individual is conformed in technology to anonymity. And, indeed, anonymity is effectively what Foucault means by training. In the Panopticon the purpose of training is to create the anonymous individual. Training makes the individual a mechanism of repetition.

Thus, to Foucault, who probably developed his critique of technology on the basis of Heidegger,[8] machines are not things generally that manufacture commodities; they are functions particularly that preserve an environment of productivity by means of repetition.

Foucault's archive seems particularly analogous to Martial Canterel's glass display unit, for the unit as such frames the totality of events held within its restrictive conditions. And even more dramatically than the

5 Ibid., 14.
6 See Deleuze, *Difference and Repetition.*
7 Ibid., 70.
8 One of the best essays on the influence of Heidegger on Foucault remains S. Ijsseling, "Foucault with Heidegger," 413-24. Ijsseling confidently believes that the text of greatest impact on Foucault was Heidegger's "Age of the World Picture."

Panopticon, the "resurrectine" invokes the whole notion of the archive *episteme* – its strategy of repetition. This fluid acts to manifest the order of events. It adds stability, rigour, and animation to the body it has enlivened. It is the element that permits or sustains a whole set of interactive relationships: a body in relation to objects, an event and location in relation to a historical context, repeated acts in relation to time and meaning. The whole scene displays a flow of power across and through a body as its memory and its reason to be.

Archivist theology, which I am presently restricting to one aspect called archaeological theology, can take some cues from Roussel. It might be noted that within the glass unit there is no outside for the participant. Only the invited guests are privileged to hold the event as an object, but necessarily they stand outside the display as observers. Inside the unit, however, the corpse is wholly caught up in its activity. It cannot transcend the condition of its actual practice, which means that its experience is one of "outsidelessness";[9] it can experience "meaning" and "deliberation" and "purpose" only as the condition of being present in actual events. The reasoning and sense of the activity inspired by resurrectine is justified in relation to the memory of being in life, being in a situation, being in the flow of power, or being in the drama of meaning. The corpse displays the tautology of an archive; an event ineluctably assumes the justification of the productivity in which it is produced. Roussel's observers cannot share the context of the corpse, but they must assume that the tautology in which it is caught works. That is, the observers must assume that the enacted memory is founded upon a system that has by way of its power relationships manufactured the conditions of a memorable act.

In place of the traditional defence of theological concepts, archaeological theology investigates the theological display. It questions how concepts emerge as events. It seeks to account for how metaphysical notions are ineluctably caught in the *produced* and *permitted* spaces of any given situation. We have already clarified this understanding by linking the form of the concept of God as an archive product to the social teleological condition of the archive in question and to its resolution (side effect), but now we can add that the God concept is a "statement" and a "perception" only because the archive *episteme*

---

9 To my knowledge Cuppitt more or less invented this term to express something similar to what Heidegger intended with "historicity."

encourages it as repetition. The God concept is an *epistemic* side effect of a system of repetition; in this sense, the effects of the system, like the figures in Roussel's glass cages, are anonymous or even mindless. Side effects, like reverberations or echoes of the constriction of possibility, return to the scene of the statement-event as its justification and its ground. I have linked this return to light-being (to what philosophy normally calls perception) as an ineluctable complement of the statement, which is why the side effect, regardless of its fictive status, still "makes sense" in terms of the system in question; it is linked inextricably to a location in a power matrix that produces the spaces of experience through the active forms of an archive. Stated plainly, the side effect "works" inside a permitted space of credibility.

CHANGING THE QUESTION

Archaeological theology separates itself from the normal tradition of systematic theology by substituting for the question of the identity of God the problem of the archival production of metaphysical concepts. Second, it situates the specific problem of the God concept in the functions of repetition. By means of repetition, the archive trains certain forms of perception within its permitted boundaries: it releases to the location a persuasive resolution. These very acts of productivity shape (that is, produce persuasive locations of) metaphysical impressions that can take (and that Western history has accepted as) the form of a God concept. We may, then, from here on appropriately call the God concept a God-form.[10]

To be sure, like the bodies injected with resurrectine, archaeological theology operates within a tautological condition. Since an archival side effect is also the grounding justification of repetition, the activity involved in this identification necessarily participates in the activity in question. What advantages archaeological theology is not a magical escape route but

---

10 This term is not a novel one since it appears in many and varied contexts in philosophical theology (and is certainly not restricted to this discipline); however, we may link it specifically to Foucault if we understand it to mean not a meta-narrative (that is, a "formation" of God or symbol of God) but an effect or ghost of linguistic operations. In this Foucauldian sense it is a fictional form or form-product much the same as the self-reflecting self described in the Panopticon analogy. I use the hyphenated expression, "God-form," to indicate the distinction from a concept of God (an idea of God) and to place emphasis on the production of a God concept.

its ability to grasp this most difficult hermeneutical problem. Traditional theology holds few analytical tools to accomplish this task since it has no account of archival side effects and no understanding of how a metaphysical concept can emerge fictively as a credible event. Archaeological theology holds the keys of this breakthrough, which is both a genuine and a decisive step beyond the normal theological tradition of the study of (the *logos* of) the divine. The new question not only brackets the question "about" God, but also turns the question upside down. Instead of presupposing God in the a priori tradition of the noumenal, the concern now is how the operation of an archive consequentially impresses metaphysical concepts into practical experience as foundational or credible forms – even when the credible form in question is a God-form.

Roussel's story helps display the contrast between normal theology and archaeological theology by means of the archival condition of "no outside." Don Cupitt, as purposefully and playfully as any theologian has, describes this situation well. "We do best to picture the world at large as a beginningless, endless, and outsideless stream of language-formed events that continually pours forth and passes away – and this noise you hear is a typical bit of it."[11] What Foucault's thinking adds to Cupitt is the problem of power: language functions to produce locations of specific horizons and limitations, which in turn account for side effects grounding perceptual credibility. Yet, Cupitt's comments accurately portray a basic archival insight. One cannot choose to belong or not belong to an archive. One is simply in it. Equally, since one can look only from the vantage point of an active archive upon the remains of another, the condition of the active archive is constantly present interpretatively as the gaze. The perpetual problem of the normal tradition of theology, in light of archaeology, is then twofold. One aspect is its long-standing attempt to bypass the condition of outsidelessness through an appeal to pure transcendentalism. The second is its inability to formulate the problem of historicity (of being in the archive) as both the problem of persuasive locations and credible resolutions.

OVERCOMING THEOLOGICAL NORMALCY

When attempting to address the first aspect, the normal tradition defaults to a Western resolution form. It presents this world, in

11 Cupitt, *Is Nothing Sacred?*, 53.

Cupitt's vivid expression, as a "photo-copy" of an original, hidden world. Apologetically, it undertakes to contrast the original to the copy, occasionally criticizing the copy in light of the original, and very often holding forward the original as the purpose and the point of the copy.

This resolution was seen in the Tillich example where theological insight is gained by positing the ground of Being (the *ov*) before the appearance of being (the ontic), and thus the apologetic task is to correct human insight by measuring it against this pure transcendental ground. The normal tradition, in effect, is prepared to rest its case on ontological foundations, but the archivist does the opposite by insisting that ontology is an impression of epistemology. Attempts to establish the foundation of experience by, in some manner, bypassing experience, an archivist upholds, is already the function, if not the effect, of the active *episteme*. The supposed security of ontology inevitably assumes machines of repetition, orders of statements, relationships of force, and spaces of permission. The normal tradition has no means to account for such productivity and no analytical language by which to contemplate the impression of side effects. Essentially, the normal tradition substitutes transcendental ideas for local products and, in this, limits the study of theology unnecessarily to assumed and unaddressed archival resolutions.

The second difficulty with the normal tradition involves understanding repetition as a theological problem. In the archive, the function of repetition is persuasion. As the Panopticon demonstrated, repetition creates the epistemological environment in which credibility emerges in the situation as its horizon (its project or what I am calling the resolution). The projecting of credibility from the location to the horizon was accounted for in the factor of social teleology where, we saw, the whole coordination of an archive and its dynamic motion engenders its own reason to be. But since the social teleological dimension of an archive depends upon the capacity of an archive to render consistently to a location the production of events, that coordination is necessarily repetition.

When the concept of God is comprehended as an archive event that emerges from the side effect of statements, the archivist is claiming that theology has no "real" ground. Rather, the theological enterprise rests on the capacity of a side effect to be repeated. In this sense archaeological theology conceives theology fictionally, but it is "functional fiction" or even "working fiction" as an archive resolution event.

Although religious concepts have no ground, they may still have value inasmuch as they are an archive form and thus potentially a site of archival transformation. Don Cupitt once again is one of the few theologians who grasps this basic struggle. He makes the distinction between the "realism" of the apologetic tradition (in which discourse refers to reality as a photocopy refers to an original) and the "non-realism" (or sometimes he uses Nietzsche's term "anti-realism") of post-structuralism. In non-realism, "Meaning and truth exist only where *we* have constituted them," and "while our human cultural forms – our language, our theories, and so on – do indeed give us access to a world, the world they open up to us is inevitably just a human-ly-constituted world."[12] Archaeological theology is consistent with Cupitt's insight but more complex in its examination of metaphysical perception related to a system of repetition.

Repetition, meanwhile, is nowhere in sight, at least analytically, as a problem for consideration in normal systematic theology. Instead, traditional theology, as Cupitt also charges, preserves the realist illusion, and this is the case even in its "postmodern" forms. Though theologians such as Mark C. Taylor, Charles Winquist, and even the conservative Jean-Luc Marion can affirm the "death of God" (the "death" of the platonic transcendental signifier and thus the death of stability, identity, and teleology), there still rings in theological forms of postmodernism a realist-like attachment to deconstruction. That is, the analysis used to justify if not perform deconstruction holds a type of outside status emerging as if *ex nihilo*, like the voice of God in an Exodus narrative or an actor *ex machina* in an ancient Greek tragedy.

No less a theologian than Taylor, who brilliantly employs the para-doxes of deconstructionist expression, portrays postmodern theology as theology at the limit where the "sacred" stands but where the sacred also denies God. Consequently Taylor explains that the post-modern theological experience is not about the dwelling place of God, which is the ancient sense of the sacred, but the abandonment of God – the God who is no-thing, who is dis-located, and who is the erring of the endlessly nomadic. As Taylor describes, "abandoned,

12 Ibid., 50.

deserted, the boundless space of the desert is no longer the place where God is encountered or the sacred experienced. The sacred abandons all encounter, deserts all experience, leaving only limitless sands where one is pushed to the limit that is never experienced."[13] This is theology that plays with nothing in contrasts and contradictions, using the art of Derridian deconstruction, to arrive at the crescendo of the expressive im-possibility (the simultaneous presence and absence) of God. It delivers language to its limit by upholding the emptiness of the signified and, in this, bringing theology to the celebration of the impossible, which is, finally, silence. At the limit, Taylor says, "I respond by not responding."[14]

Taylor's postmodern expression is no doubt artful, insightful, and at times deliberately camouflaged. He brings language to a type of dead end where God is reached at the limit of what is not or at least no longer. Still, from an archivist point of view, the situation is not as ironic as Taylor may assume. Can any theologian, by the sheer employment of linguistic art, suddenly stand at a limit set outside an archive permission? The archivist must rather uphold that whether one speaks of postmodern liberals or postmodern conservatives, the attempts to escape the condition of being present in an archive by an obvious appeal either to transcendentalism (the conservative choice) or the subtle dance with nothingness and absence (the liberal or radical choice) neither acknowledges nor incorporates the very machinery that produces such a location as an event. Marion appeals to transcendentalism with his *ex nihilo* pretensions and Taylor avoids the problem of transcendence with the dance of nothingness, but neither encounters the question of the permission of their theological claims. Each attempts to exhaust language in order to escape to the limit, that is, to achieve an "outside" point of critique, but the attempt can only yield an ironic return since each must stand in the archive holding the presumptions of the side effect accomplishment. Each participates in the constriction of possibility.

An archivist theology recognizes that it participates in its own production, its narration is its own creation, and the fundamental task of archaeological theology includes the full recognition of its own permission within an epistemic location. It does not attempt to escape to

---

13 Taylor, *About Religion*, 45.
14 Ibid., 47.

an outside location in either traditional or radical ways. It trumps the apologetic tradition in both its conservative and radical forms. Its question remains the production of God-forms, not the (in)defence of God.

OBJECTIONS AND DIRECTIVES
TO NEW UNDERSTANDINGS

What I have presented as the normal or apologetic tradition of systematic theology can issue one poignant objection from the side of its radical expression: namely, if God is conceived in the archive as "permission" formed through varying constructs of history, is not God then reduced to a transcendental reflection of the self? It seems that individuals framed in an archive merely compose a conceptual horizon and name it God, but the referent in the end is only the projecting image of the self from a location of permission. Isn't this a restatement of what was already accomplished in the nineteenth century with Ludwig Feuerbach and the so-called "Young Hegelians"?[15] Where then is the novelty of the new expression?

Archaeological theology unfolds by examining the archive *episteme*, and it could be claimed that since the *episteme* is effectively the expressed strategies of statements, then the very notion of the archaeology of knowledge is consistent with a classical analysis like Feuerbach's. The rational structure of the human mind, one might claim, accounts for the nature of the project on the horizon. Particularly, it accounts for the perfections (wisdom, love, justice) that Feuerbach argued are cast upon the canvas of history as a horizon called God.

Feuerbach's conclusion is based on his assertion that the predicate is the true subject.[16] He means that what is attributed to the divine as its predicate (such as supreme love) only reflects the inverse of what resides negatively in the human subject, for the human being is finite and incapable of reaching such an ideal. So, the divine becomes a type of super-human predicate projected from the merely human subject. God takes the form of supreme love from transcendental human self-awareness. God is the prototypical perfect human or

---

15 Feuerbach, *The Essence of Christianity.* Among the Young Hegelians were Ludwig Feuerbach, Karl Marx, David Friedrich Strauss, and Bruno Bauer.

16 Ibid., 99.

humanity writ large. Humans deny to themselves only what they attribute to God, according to Feuerbach.[17]

But archaeological theology does not hold the same structure of
argumentation as that forwarded by Feuerbach and later used by
Nietzsche. To begin, the claim is different, and, equally, both the intention and conclusion are different as well. Feuerbach sought to
capture for humanity its true essence that, for centuries, had been
projected upon God and held captive by religion. He sought in genuine Enlightenment fashion to liberate human nature from ecclesiastical custody and deliver humanity back to itself in moral freedom.
He shared this vision with David Friedrich Strauss, and in a general
sense his thought defined the amazingly progressive spirit of late
nineteenth-century theology. But archaeological theology does not
assume that there can be an essence to human nature, and it does
not contend that God is only the positive predicate of an otherwise
weak and negative human spirit. So, in archaeological theology, God
is not the human project writ large.

To be sure, in archaeological theology, God is a human creation,
and the emergence of God is socially portrayed and anonymously
conceived in relation to human experience. In archaeological theology, there is a sense in which the God-form cannot be understood,
for it has no specific cause; it emerges ineluctably in the side effects
of the statement. What archaeological theology can do is set a different agenda that rests not on the emancipation of humanity from the
despotism of the ill-conceived but delivers the thinking of theology to
liberty with the God-form.

The challenge of archaeological theology can be outlined in three
directives. These do not pose the limits of this form of theological
investigation, but they guide the task in its initial undertakings and
help set the question for future endeavours.

The first directive is to uncover productivity. Archaeology holds no
premeditation when it claims that God is a product of the archive.
Along with Foucault, it looks at the surface, at what is there as the
resolution of the event. God is in this way a posteriori, after the fact of
an event, and only available in the permission the event performs.
The investigation focuses on the means by which forces open space to
conceptual horizons and resolve the archive in theological statements.

17 Ibid., 25–32.

When Tillich was used as an example, the question was not how to interpret his theological endeavours but how to display the way in which the structure of his thought resolved the archive in which he was engaged. This rather anonymous way of approaching the question of God is the analytical directive of archaeological theology.

The second directive is related to forms of resolution. The archivist is not seeking to define or defend a certain concept of reality. In other words, there is no apologetic task involved. Rather the question is how certain concepts are permitted in the archive and, as such, may even be desired or willed or comprehended as necessity. This analysis involved portraying the social teleological structure of the statement and the resolution of the statement in its side effects. In the Panopticon, resolution was portrayed as the self-transcending self who is a product of the forces of inwardness and training. In archaeological theology, the interest therefore lies not in what is revealed but in what is resolved. The second directive, then, consists of displaying resolution.

The third directive is the location. With emphasis on the question of resolution, the investigation of archaeological theology remains focused on understanding what produces the statement of God as an event. This brings the importance of location immediately forward, for the analysis of the production of space is needed to uncover how the specific event is opened as permission and resolution. What dynamics of performance constitute the space and what creates it as "this space," that is, as this conjunction or set of relationships? Foucault imaginatively describes space as heterotopias in which the crossing of forces, the synchrony and disconnect of statements, the reasoning of gestures or compulsions, the functions of contrast, etc., form the composite moment.[18] The emphasis on the location – and on the production of the location – marks the determined recognition that theology can no longer go forward in the guises of transcendental escapism. Rather, it must reconcile itself to outsidelessness; it must see itself as an event. Archaeological theology is built on the critical uncovering of the God-form as event.

18 The original article has appeared variously in English as "On Other Spaces" or "Of Other Spaces," but my comments are derived from the original, Foucault, "Des espaces autre," 46–9.

Archaeological theology is one style of thinking inspired by Michel Foucault but by no means the only one. Archaeology directs the theological question explicitly to the historical forms of concepts and the intimate construction of their sense. However, there can be another task, which is the inversion of theology. Inversion presents theology as the task of thinking at variance in an archive. It is the work of genealogical theology.

BECAUSE IT IS BEING PLAYD
THERE ON A FALSE PREMISE

10

no evidence up

Genealogical Theology

IF THE GOD CONCEPT can be described as a form emerging in archival operations, if it can be displayed as an ineluctable side effect of
the event of the statement, a natural question concerns the future of
theology as a study, and its point. In archaeological theology, the
quest is to uncover the social teleological circulation of power in order to account for an archive's metaphysical resolution. In its activity,
it renders the God-form fictional and dismisses the question of the
existence of God as both misleading and misdirected. The question
is not whether God exists but what function the God-form plays and
how that form is involved in archive productivity. This suggests the all
too familiar nihilism of postmodern thought. "God is a product,"
after all, is not too dissimilar to "God is dead" and perhaps reaches
the same conclusion: *requiem aeternam deo*.[1]

Yet, the point has not been to conclude that theology is useless.
Neither is the present study satisfied with the conclusion of Nietzsche's
famous dictum. Instead, an investigation of the archive delivers the
surprising conclusion that theology is helpful in understanding archive side effects, the emergence of these fictional statement-events,
and their productive power. Second, archival theology is about presence at a "location," for it is not possible to be in an archive without
also being in a constriction of possibility and thus participating in a
teleological resolution.

If the substantial point in archaeological theology is to investigate
the emergence of religious ideas in an archive and how they form in
the archive as its desired end, its *telos*, and its resolution, then a second

1 Nietzsche, *The Gay Science*, 126.

kind of theological task is possible if one introduces transgression to
the question of the archive and its operation. This latter task can be
presented as the task of archive inversion, which is part of genealogical theology.

GENEALOGICAL THEOLOGY AS CRITICAL PRESENCE

Genealogical theology arises from the irony deeply lodged in archaeological theology. That irony involves the way archaeological
theology affirms itself as a location in the productivity of an archive.
It is very capable of recognizing itself as permission. Genealogical
theology is a more difficult expression that arises out of this basic
condition of irony. What genealogy seeks to do is invert its location in
the archive as if a type of non-resolvable presence. The act of inversion is transgression, and it means that in the archive it is possible to
stand as difference in relation to repetition.

To stand in difference to repetition is to be as a non-event in relation to an event. In the constriction of possibility, the event is permissible because it is repetition, but equally the constriction has excluded
what we might call the unrepeatable. The excluded is the disqualified
or simply the non-event. In panopticism the disqualified are those
delinquent elements oriented differently from the teleological reading of the carceral society. They are as transgressive non-events in
relation to the side effect of the perception norm. As transgressive
non-events, accordingly, they are "difference" that the side effects
constitute as the project of overcoming. Delinquency in panopticism is a project of overcoming resolved in the side effect of the self-
transcending self.

We can see then that the "non-event" turns, as it were, on a second
level of irony not available to archaeological investigation. This second level consists of the irony of using the archive project to be permanent difference within the project of overcoming. Being in
permanent difference cannot occur in spite of the archive operation
but because of it, for it is "difference" located in repetition or difference that receives its permission from repetition. Thus, transgression
in the archive is irony because it is difference permitted by the productivity of the same.

In the archive, difference is an orientation to the non-event: it consists of taking advantage of the location by retreating from its

permission. As a deliberate orientation from a location to its non-event, genealogical theology is also a permanent condition of self-contradiction. In the act of grasping itself it necessarily loses itself. It must do so if it is to be the transgressive location, for the act of inversion in the archive is the contradiction of productivity. It is the act of giving the location away to nothing.

To these difficult expressions there must still be one element added. The orientation to the non-event cannot be achieved outside of archival permission. This point needs to be underlined because the archivist must avoid the tempting conclusion that somehow hermeneutical problems have been avoided or theology can, by means of transgression, discover a new route to the noumenal. On the contrary, the orientation depends on the accomplishment of the archive. Even though a transgressive orientation is engaged from the archive, it is an "inversion" of the event because, as Deleuze would say, it is *the outside of the inside.*

The practice of genealogical theology can be called the practice of "critical presence" in the archive. This describes the awareness of being in a location, which is a critical awareness of production, and the manner in which transgression is presence because it is not repetition. To use Heideggerian terms, transgression is presence precisely because it is not "everydayness" or "forgetting" or the "they."[2] In contrast to the tradition of normal theology aligning presence to transcendentalism, genealogical theology holds that presence is absence.

For the transgressive orientation to be radically maintained its activity must be the permanent concern of absence. It must not merely concern what has not occurred in the archive but rather *what cannot occur* in the archive. This distinction is necessary for two reasons. One is that transgression cannot be confused with wistfulness or yearning. It is not the basis of hope for progress or the determination of perseverance in the short term for greater gains in the long term. To be sure, hope and perseverance are admirable human qualities and significant questions in theology, but they are not the task of transgression. Neither is transgression understood correctly as a vehicle to inspire social reform in an archive or a call for a retreat to capture lost potential. Insofar as transgression is understood in these ways, it has been returned to thematic contemplation – or to an apologetic

2 Heidegger, *Being and Time.*

function – and has forsaken the challenge of genealogy. Rather, genealogical theology is permanently in favour of an orientation toward the non-event as *actual presence*. Genealogical theology is about what *is not* in permission and what *is not* in resolution. It is about the presence of not being. It is the inverse of the theme, the resistance to resolution, the negation of apology, and actual presence by means of the non-event.

Because transgression in genealogical theology can sound so much like simple negation, it will be helpful to distinguish it from the Christian tradition of negative theology.

GENEALOGY AND NEGATIVE THEOLOGY

Negative theology in Christianity is based on the *via negativa* or negative path defined in medieval scholasticism and carried forward to the modern era. The *via negativa* tradition tends to defy definition precisely because it negates the positive attributes of a theological system in an attempt to find unity with God in mysticism and in silence. The *via negativa* tradition disqualifies definite theological statements as if idols that cover final darkness and the ineffable mysterious called God. One might well ask what, then, could be more fitting for genealogical theology and its orientation to the non-event than the *via negativa*?

The difficulty is that the *via negativa* remains an apologetic form of theology. Though conceived to complement the positive accomplishments of Christian doctrine (and historically it is regarded suspiciously by the Church only when it fails this task as in, for example, the case of Meister Eckhart), the *via negativa* is like an antidote to taking doctrines of faith too literally. Every doctrine necessarily falls short of the reality of God, for God could hardly be the absolute if this were not so, and the negative path ensures the eclipse of propositions based on human reason. Still, the negative path plays a positive dogmatic role since it delivers the believer from ignorance to "faith" (or trust) in the transcendental oneness that dogma (however inadequately) represents. Historically, then, the aim of the *via negativa* is to complement a *via positiva* by leading to "faith" in the dogmatically defined "mysteries" of doctrine.

Despite appearances to the contrary, the *via negativa* is an archive resolution event for it merely recedes the resolution of the archive as a constantly extended *telos*. If the positive claim is to attribute omnipotence to God, the negation of omnipotence is only to conclude that God extends beyond the conceptual limits of power. Thus, in this way, the negative tradition overwhelmingly opens the positive resolution of the archive as desire by the perpetual extension of the resolution to the archive horizon. The *via negativa* eclipses the statement but does so in order to strengthen it all the more. The *via negativa*, then, is resolutely not an encounter with nothingness, and its method is nowhere near the practices of genealogical theology.

In contrast to traditional negative theology, genealogy grasps itself both with greater dynamism and greater subtlety. It is not about naming a limit and then defending theology as revelation perpetually extended beyond the limit but about opening a reversal in the immediate archival experience – in the present here and now. Genealogy is not attempting to surpass an archive; it is an attempt to be outside within the archive. And while the *via negativa* includes the affirmation of ontology, for it is based on God's perfection as infinitely receding being, the content of genealogy is the transgression of teleology. Transgression as an activity of genealogy cannot be approached through the *via negativa* and its emphasis on limits. Rather, transgression discovers limits in order to counter-act them. This is why it must be thought of as a reversal rather than an overcoming.

These thoughts can be called Foucauldian because they reflect Foucault's often quoted critique of the Enlightenment. To Foucault, Kant sought to discover the limits of thinking in order to hold reason within them whereas "the point, in brief, is to transform the critique [of Kant that was] conducted in the form of necessary limitations into a practical critique that takes the form of a possible transgression."[3] The transgression of limits is the fundamental act of genealogy.

In modern times, the *via negativa* is more properly called negative theology and its most radical expression was the Death of God. It is theology expressed as the child of Nietzsche. When it is said that genealogical theology is an orientation toward non-events or nothingness and that the only absolute involved is its own presence, a perceptive reader will wish to push the question into and beyond the modern forms of negative theology. For negative theology too speaks

3 Foucault, *The Foucault Reader*, 45.

of the fabrication of horizons and affirms the total presence of the moment.[4]

Negative theology expresses the collapse or death of the transcendental world that, for centuries of Western history, was the domain of an absolute God and "his" universal ideas. These universals included what in this study have been called archive side effects such as ontology and teleology. The collapse of the ideal world was often described as the emptying (*kenosis*) of the heavens (or the spirit of God) into the history of humanity. The whole movement called negative theology became a clarion call, one of the most significant of Christian history, for the theology of suffering (the crucified God) and for liberation theology (the preferential option for the poor).[5] Negative theology, by its ability to critique the tradition of transcendentalism, was able to counter-act the history of the aseity (and equally asceticism) of God with dynamic notions of praxis and compassion. Any critique of negative theology ought not to be at the expense of its insight and the courage of many great theologians.

While negative theology rejected the transcendental categories that defined, if not protected, God, its shortcoming lay in its failure to account for the presence and persistence of transcendental categories in history. Because of this, it remained unable to guard against a return, after its initial period of radicalism, of new forms of orthodoxy and new engagements of normal theological practices.[6] Genealogical theology, because it emerges from the already articulated archaeological theology, can understand transcendental categories as side effects in the archive and can seize a sense of social responsibility for their (humanly produced) forms. Genealogical theology does not reject the transcendental tradition of theology but transforms the relationship of the theologian to it from apology to

4 As an example, see Altizer, *Total Presence.*

5 Miranda, *Being and the Messiah.*

6 William Hamilton is a case in point. As a founder of the Death of God movement in North America, he reverted back to normal Christian theology with his rejection of postmodern theology, new historical Jesus scholarship, and the re-evaluation of the so-called "Western canon." Hamilton seeks a literary "Jesus" who remains primarily a dying and rising "symbol" of an essentially Christian understanding of the human condition celebrated in poetry, art, drama, and all things other than philosophy and theology. Hamilton, *A Quest for the Post-Historical Jesus.*

transgression, from a priori to construction, and from abstraction to critical presence.

Genealogical theology has the advantage of already comprehending the transcendental tradition critically, yet its solution is not pure rejection. The point is to account for rather than empty the transcendental categories. In this act it grasps the problem of the archive rather than, as in negative theology, purging itself from the processes that produce it. Genealogy takes advantage of the archive rather than seeking escape. Unlike negative theology, it keeps itself from the inadvertent return to the normal tradition.

Foucault exemplifies the practice of genealogical theology when he challenged France's prison system. His intentions were not limited to prison reform, the amelioration of prison conditions, or the defence of the rights of prisoners.[7] Neither were his acts equivalent to those of an anarchist. His quest, rather, from within the socio-political fact, was to place himself strategically in orientation toward the non-event of the "carceral" archive. Foucault sought to transgress the very structures of the project-reasoning (or the social teleological resolution) of the prison's existence. In this, we saw, he understood delinquency as a product of the carceral society. The "delinquent" merely demonstrates to the carceral order the justification of its own existence. When Foucault spoke of a "carceral continuum"[8] and the "carceral system,"[9] both terms reflected a most poignant conclusion: "the circuit of delinquency would seem to be not the sub-product of a prison which, while punishing, does not succeed in correcting; it is rather the direct effect of a penalty which, in order to control illegal practices, seems to invest certain of them in a mechanism of 'punishment-reproduction,' of which imprisonment is one of the main parts."[10] Foucault actively promotes a breech with the society of delinquency production. He seeks the frustration of an ethical order that produces rather than addresses the social question. He wants counter-ethics, and to achieve this goal he employs his location ironically as a productive site of counter-productivity.

7 Foucault was involved in the founding of the Groupe d'information sur les prisons with Daniel Defert, Jean-Marie Domenach, and Pierre Vidal-Naquet.

8 Foucault, *Discipline and Punish*, 303.

9 Ibid., 301.

10 Ibid., 282-3.

Foucault created of himself a critical presence by his transgressive orientation. This opened to him the permanent activity of *being other* within the production of *being in* the archive. Foucault took up the fact of his positive presence in the archive as simultaneously an inversion of the archive order. By doing so he could later speak of a project of the self: a self who is authentic by being permanently other. It is with this same gesture that genealogical theology proposes its liberating agenda.

Born out of an orientation to the non-event conceived as archival inversion, genealogical theology holds a certain freedom or liberation in relation to the archive order. Of course, this "orientation" remains conditional; of course, it remains inside the archive. But it may anticipate its presence in the archive as frustration rather than resolution. It is the "other" in relation to the teleological system, and thus its act of being present is the act of frustrating the produced resolution of the archive condition. Genealogical theology liberates the Christian theological tradition from its history of hibernation in apology. Whereas normal theology defends the permission from which it is constructed, transgression occurs as the frustration of what is permitted.

Again, if theology is to remain critical, it must understand the irony upon which it rests. While transgression frustrates the actually permitted, it is almost as if a type of fate were at work insofar as its activity is always carried out with the normal. It can transgress only by defying what is already productively available. It must be other to what has created it and what orients it. Genealogical theology needs to affirm its historic setting as that which holds the inversion of its orientation to the non-event. Its sense of liberation can only be earned within the problem of the archive.

Still, without the notion of transgression, there can be no sense to the archive at all. First, there can be no understanding of archival transformations if not for collapses, negations, and shifts. These necessitate an understanding of an archive as a system of repetition that alters or becomes a new archive when the order of repetition cannot be fulfilled. When panopticism cannot be understood as training, when carceral acts cannot be understood as reformatory, or when punishment cannot be understood as justice, the order of repetition will collapse, an outside will invade, and a redistribution of statements and re-seeing of events will occur. Genealogical theology offers no different analysis: the normal tradition is present as a resolution produced in the side effect of archival events. The point of inverting locations, of finding fissures in the armour of repetition, or of being "other" as a form of "presence" in the archive is to enact transformation. Genealogical theology plays with transformation inasmuch as it frustrates resolution.

Archaeological theology first presented theology as an expression of side effect resolutions in an archive; genealogical theology was then presented as the practice of being in the archive in a transgressive relation to the resolution uncovered in the analysis of archaeological theology. With these two aspects of theology presented in the framework of Foucauldian thought, the question now turns to the future of philosophical theology.

11

Displaying and Dwelling in the Archive

THE REVIEW OF ARCHAEOLOGICAL THEOLOGY and genealogical theology opens two questions for consideration in the context of the philosophical study of theology. One is the archaeology question about the epistemological condition of thinking theologically in the archive. This can be called the question of displaying the archive. The second question concerns the genealogical practice of being in the archive. This can be called the question of dwelling.

In light of the new accounting of metaphysical ideals as ineluctable yet phantom side effects of archive activity, the primary criticism directed against the apologetic forms of philosophical theology, which I have called normal forms, is that there is no accounting of archive productivity, of the statement-event, and of the archive resolution in social teleology. Rather, the normal tradition assumes these activities and even presents theology as their foundation. In this sense, in terms of the archivist understanding, the normal tradition is untenable. In the archive the foundation of the apologetic tradition – its secure and pre-given world order – vanishes before the dynamic effects of language-being, light-being, and statement-events. Lacking analytical tools to investigate archival activity, the normal tradition bases its theological insight on accidental effects and phantom referents.

THE RETURN OF EPISTEMOLOGICAL PRIORITY

A brief tour of the normal theological tradition would suggest that what is different in the archive is the rejection of the priority of ontology so characteristic of the Western theological heritage. Collectively, both archaeological and genealogical theology account for ontology but do so in light of the priority of epistemology.[1]

The priority of epistemology, a trademark of postmodern hermeneutics, at first can seem foreign to theology and its historic emphasis on the question of being.[2] As we discovered, in the classic presentation of Tillich, Being is the presupposition of the question of being. But Tillich is not an isolated example. Karl Rahner also presents the "unthematic" or "permanent ground" as the presupposition of the thematic.[3] In both expressions, the ontological foundation of reality is accepted as a religious a priori – a necessary and final referent generally called God. The religious a priori, in Western thought usually attributed to Schleiermacher, became the foundation of modern theological speculation. The insight, though formulated in the specificities of theological liberalism, is indeed rooted in the very fibre of theology as a philosophical enterprise.[4]

Archaeological and genealogical theology stand out from the Western tradition and appear closer to an Eastern expression due to the shift to the priority of epistemology. For in these archive

1 As Don Cupitt often points out, this shifting in the foundations of the Western experience is particularly expressed with Immanuel Kant. Still, we must admit that Kant, by way of inspiring Idealism, radically opened the question of ontology in later existentialism and phenomenology. Kant's epistemology limited the human experience to historicity, to knowledge in the condition of finiteness. Accordingly, at least in theological terms, after Kant the question of being could only be a question that invades from the outside as revelation. Heidegger waits upon being (revelation) through poetry and mysticism, not through rationalism. German Idealism, then, expressed the question of being first as the a priori of human existence, and second as that which can be signified only by means of deference (that is, poetic expression). While I do not ignore the philosophical history behind the question of being, it is a different claim to say that the question of being is an archive effect. This latter emphasis raises a new problem in theology.

2 Heidegger certainly intended to "reawaken" the "question of the meaning of being" (*Being and Time*); perhaps that very awakening encouraged, in postmodern hermeneutics, the new problem of the meaning of meaning.

3 Rahner, *Foundations of Christian Faith*, 53, 57-61.

4 Here I mean to refer to the whole problem of the one or universal substance found in the pre-Socratics as much as in Plato, Aristotle, Plotinus, and, by this journey, into early speculation about and composite language used for the Christian Trinity. Inasmuch as Heidegger stated that the question of Being was lost in the metaphysical tradition of Western philosophy, it seems equally plausible to argue that the question of Being is actually the overwhelming preoccupation of the Western philosophical tradition.

theologies, epistemology is not a problem of interpretation (not a hermeneutical situation to be overcome) but a condition; epistemology displaces ontology as the condition of existence in the archive. Epistemology alone accounts for the side effects of fictive (ideological) relationships to the world as it is. Though it makes sense, rationally, to propose an absolute, ontological foundation prior to the question of existence, which is what the normal tradition does with profundity, in the archive the problem returns to the epistemological condition in which such speculation is conceived. In other words, "being in Being" (or the presupposition of Being to the question of being) is not really a theological problem. It is rather an archive resolution statement.

This hermeneutical shift from ontology to epistemology can seem like much ado about nothing, but it is wholly appropriate to insist that it be seen against the background of Western ontological metaphysics. This normal tradition has had an overwhelming psychological impact beyond theology as the engrained habit (the myth or pattern of interpretation) of socio-cultural experience. In the thinking of Augustine, which over centuries defined the basic structures of Western philosophy, Christian ontology is expressly the doctrine of "original sin." Granted, in our time "sin" seems like a medieval relic, its signifying power remains fixed to notions of corrupted or obscured primordial conditions and authentic ways of being. The ontic human being separated from an original ontological purity remains a critical element of the analytical characteristics of Western psychological and theological thought.

This basic structure remains evident in the most accomplished statements of Western theology. Sin as the condition of being primordially separated from wholeness is theologically the finite limitation of ideal or absolute freedom. The contradiction of finiteness and freedom defines the human condition as one of sin. Thus, Reinhold Niebuhr explained that human beings are "insecure and involved in natural contingency" and they seek to overcome their "insecurity by a will-to-power which overreaches the limits of human creatureliness."[5] Or in Tillich, "destiny has the character of necessity"; thus, human beings live in freedom but with the restriction of destiny: "freedom

5 Niebuhr, *The Nature and Destiny of Man*, 178.

and destiny limit each other." Human beings have "finite freedom."[6]
Or David Tracy; "we cannot logically say that each human being *must*
sin with metaphysical necessity save at the unwelcome logical and
theological price of destroying the reality of individual freedom. And
yet, the tradition argued, each human being is responsible for the
fact that eventually, indeed inevitably, he or she does personally sin."
The point here is that the tradition upholds that craving or desire for
wholeness occurs within contingent historical circumstances and that
this contingency is an ontological fact. Sin is not primarily guilt or
malevolence but consequential of self-deceiving behaviour that substitutes partiality for wholeness.

If the tradition of original sin as the human condition is explained
in a more philosophical way, it can be said that the human condition
consists of the separation between the subjective freedom of an individual and the objective setting in which individuality is mediated
both to the self and the world.[7] Therefore, in this sense, when philosophical theology speaks of separation, more than an existential condition it is also including a social reality and the question of a just
society, for "guilt" is the condition of being in the world as the responsible subject who nevertheless is always lost to itself by means of
the mediating role of the necessary setting in history. Christianity in
its normal expression has with great sophistication developed, over
its long history, a political, social, and psychological analytic founded
on this distinctive understanding of sin as ontological separation. It
has also, in its expressed Christology and Eschatology, comprehended
the resolution to separation not as an individual achievement but as
the action of the "other" (the divine mystery) giving itself over to
existence (that is, to history and time) as radical acceptance ("grace").
The popular term for this theology is "fall and redemption," but in
effect this names only a pattern or movement that is ontologically
intended. It concerns original Being overcoming the separation of
being from Being.

It should be evident, then, that the challenge involved in presenting an alternative to an overwhelming and ontologically based

6 Tillich, *Systematic Theology* 2: 32.

7 Though I am not referring to a particular individual but expressing an understanding of the theological tradition, the reader may not be surprised that the understanding expressed in this paragraph is influenced by the philosophy of Sartre, *Being
and Nothingness*.

metaphysical tradition is not a mere option offered lightly in the mix of philosophical speculation. The emergence of epistemology as the primary question, which can be identified with Hume and Kant but which in the thought of Foucault has taken a radical advance, is a genuine shifting of momentum in the historic direction of Western thought. And, as the reception given the work of Foucault indicates, the shift seems to know few limits in terms of the subjects affected. Theology and theological speculation are relative latecomers to this otherwise remarkable occasion.

When the question of the future of theology is raised in light of archaeological and genealogical theologies, that is, in light of epistemologically based theologies, beyond being a "questioning" and a "proposing," it is indeed a genuine opening to new directions. To lift the tradition from its ontological anchor is equally to name a new mythology.[8] It is significant to explore, however tentatively, the prospective character of these new directions.

ARCHAEOLOGY AS EPISTEMOLOGICAL EMPTINESS

If theology accepts the epistemological priority – if theology accepts itself as an unsubstantiated product of archival forces – it has no choice but to place the problem of itself and its historic usefulness in a different setting. It has to come to terms with itself on the basis of a different mythology. The task of theology is no longer revelation; it does not involve anymore the lifting of the curtain to expose the backstage (or ground) of "being." There is no "backstage" or depth or profundity or authenticity or purity in the linguistic composition of reality. There are only side effects that promote this impression as the resolution of the event. This is essentially how the Panopticon was presented, the side effect being the modern self-transcending self who resolves enclosure with training.

The structure and sense of the concept of God, then, is consequential of the historic-linguistic coincidences that position side effects, that generate teleological impressions, and that create meaning within the composition of archival forces. The strength of archaeological theology lies in accepting its epistemological condition and even promoting this condition as its advantage. Archaeological theology is not

8 By "mythology" here I mean an extensive shift in world view.

about uncovering a hidden truth that has escaped the history of theological reflection but rather about exposing the socio-teleological structures that manufacture the fiction of truth claims. In this sense the advantage of archaeological theology is its emptiness. As Nietzsche might say, its presupposition is "finite force."[9] Archaeological theology claims to be useful only at the phenomenal level of investigation. Like Foucault's archaeology, the ground is the surface.

Foucault posed the question, "What is this specific existence that emerges from what is said and nowhere else?"[10] Archaeological theology offers to transform the question into asking how a particularly structured God-form makes its appearance in an archive. What accounts for the event of a God-form? Archaeological theology in a curious way is not about theology but about accounting for it; it is empty insofar as its intention is limited to the display rather than defence of the question of theology.

Archaeological theology can be censured for its outwardly presumptive ground, for obviously it too must be a product of an archive. The charge of presumption however is not as devastating as might be imagined because, despite appearances, it is not really a pertinent observation. Every inquiry holds a similar problem. Every subject of every inquiry gains definition from the methodologies used to apply it. This is now an understanding of venerable age,[11] and indeed archaeological analysis actually accounts for this basic hermeneutical condition with admirable ease. But further, although one must grant that archaeological theology is a phenomenon within an archive, it does not follow that, as such, it is irrelevant to the analysis of an archive. Being in an archive does not falsify the analysis of an archive. On the contrary, one should rather say that investigating an archive is only possible on the basis of admitting one is in an archive. Consequently, archaeology is highly relevant to understanding even itself *precisely because* it admits it is a product; an archive "product" is exactly after the fact of an archive operation and therefore necessarily inclusive of the comprehensibility of that operation. The very admission that it is an archive product offers archaeological theology a

9 Nietzsche, *The Will to Power*, 324.

10 Foucault, *Archaeology of Knowledge*, 28.

11 This basic insight can be related to Giambattista Vico and his *New Science* (1725), which influenced modern notion of historicism.

certain liberty of approach to the question of theological productivity. Its strength is its focus on linguistic evidence and not on the general assumption of a "spirit of the times."[12]

The analysis, then, when cast against the background of the tradition, emerges from the fact that archaeological theology affirms no
transcendental ground. It claims instead that religion only objectifies
the archival side effect. A side effect has no tie to a transcendental
anchor, and it can be explained wholly without it. Archaeological
theology does not ground itself outside an archive order, and need
not think it can, to display the order under question. It works in an
archive seeking the effect of archives. It is a phenomenal rather than
noumenal theology; it is re-presenting the surface rather than signifying the depth.

Even further, beyond its quest to display, archaeological theology
names the predicament that archaeological analysis has brought to
the fore. It might be thought that this "predicament" is a "postmodern
breakthrough" – at least, a breakthrough in the Western tradition. For
Western theological thought has been embedded in the teleological
productivity of its archive, so much so that Western theology is truly
"eschatological" in definition. Zoroastrianism, Judaism, Christianity,
and Islam all share this element of linear history directed to an end in
contrast to the Eastern (and the earlier Western Pagan) emphasis on
circular history destined to repeat. Archaeological analysis breaks free
from the traditional base of eschatology because it is able to comprehend the archive as an anonymous or indifferent activity. As a system
of productivity, the archive generates effects but it does not have a
purpose;[13] the archive is simultaneously full of activity and empty of
significance. True, this has to be expressed with subtle understanding,
for it must be granted that the archive produces its own horizon, and
in this sense, over time, it is accumulative in the sense that "it constitutes its own past."[14] But this does not mean that out of the momentum of accumulation there lies ahead a promised "dawn about to
return";[15] rather, the accumulation of statements creates the limits of

12 Foucault, *Archaeology of Knowledge*, 15.

13 "Purpose" may not be the best word here, but I do mean "propos" or forward-
ness or aim. An archive has "purpose" (function) in the sense that it works to coordinate events summarily as "reality."

14 Foucault, *Archaeology of Knowledge*, 124.

15 Ibid., 125.

the progenitive horizon: what I called the constriction of possibility. Thus, while the archive clearly produces a sense of purpose, which is its social teleological effect, there is no "end" as such to the archive. It is groundlessly active. It is empty of meaning transcendentally, though, as practical experience Foucault will tell us, it functions perfectly well. Paradoxically, then, the archive is the production of meaning as emptiness or perhaps even out of emptiness. It is an epistemic system with epistemic consequences that are called effects; its effects certainly express if even confine situational reality, but still they arise anonymously. As Kierkegaard might have said, an archive produces an illusory ground that is set upon a bottomless current, floating in the middle of nowhere.[16]

Archaeological theology, then, poses itself only as the vehicle to display the phenomenal history of religious concepts, theological expressions, and philosophical forms. It displays the metaphysical tradition but is not itself metaphysics so much as a positive explanation of why a given set of metaphysical expressions emerged as credible in their context and time. It is empty insofar as the act of displaying requires no foundation, assumes no pre-given ground, idealizes no origin or return, makes no claim about truth, and promotes no form of resolution. It is emptiness in order to display: a practical accounting for the event, but as such a form of theology the normal tradition has never accomplished.

GENEALOGY AS RELIGIOUS AIMLESSNESS

If archaeological theology is an accounting for and displaying of theological concepts in an archive, then genealogical theology concerns the practice of theology in an archive. Archaeological theology is an analytical tool divorced from teleology by means of emptiness, but genealogical theology engages an archive and practises a form of theology within it. What then is the genealogical sense of practice?

---

16 In *Stages of Life's Way*, Kierkegaard used the image of faith as swimming joyfully over 70,000 fathoms of water. The image came out of his sense of existential nihilism where, on the subjective level, there are no securities in life but only levels of trust. While I do not mean exactly the same thing, one can identify the archive function in similar ways.

Does practice mean doing theology or even performing it? Does practice approximate what Heidegger meant by "dwelling"?[17] Is it an expression borrowed from Buddhism that intends mindfulness or awakening?

The practice of genealogical theology is an ethical concern carried out in an archive according to the breakthrough of archaeological theology. But "ethics" here is not principles or norms, since such cannot be extended from archaeology, so much as awareness and presence in the archive. Genealogical theology does not proceed with the notion of purpose (*telos*) since it does not engage (or is liberated from) the archive socio-teleological condition. The analytic of archaeological theology enables the practice of genealogical theology, but this practice must be called aimless since its critique is generated in the emptiness of archaeology.

Genealogical theology, we can say, starts with "presence" or "being in" the archive, and in its way even normal theology begins here, too. Theology has always included the question of meaning and is about the quest for it. In the monotheistic traditions, the answer to the question of meaning is revelation. In the description of his method of correlation, Tillich declares, "Revelation answers questions which have been asked and always will be asked because they are 'we ourselves.'"[18] But the "we ourselves" theologically is the experience of the human limit: the limitation of knowledge and the final limit of life. Rahner makes the same claim when he states that "the real revelation discloses something which is still unknown for [hu]man[s] from the world: the inner reality of God and his personal and free relationship to spiritual creatures."[19] Revelation in the normal tradition is not intrinsic to the natural experience of humankind but arrives rather as the free movement of "God" who is outside experience yet fundamental to the possibility of experience. In a general way, the tradition expresses the human limit precisely because the proposition of revelation could not be mystery if in the end it rested only upon what is within the human condition. Even in its deconstructive forms, even in theological expressions inspired by Derrida,[20] where

---

17 Heidegger, "Building, Dwelling, Thinking."
18 Tillich, *Systematic Theology* 1: 62
19 Rahner, *Foundations*, 171.
20 Winquist, *Epiphanies of Darkness*, and Taylor, *About Religion*.

one might think a genuine theology of outsidelessness is possible (as Cupitt is able to achieve), even here theologians eagerly appeal to the revelatory *noumena* or the silence or the limit or the outside as the only aim theology can hold. Theology even in its deconstructive form articulates the normal expressions of mystically awaiting that break in silence, that promised eschatological moment, embedded in the monotheistic psyche of the Western interpretation of history. The great resolution.

Genealogical theology might include some of the traditional sense of "waiting" at the limit and, to a degree, can mean "presence" in the archive as waiting. The influence of Heidegger cannot be denied either in Foucault or in genealogy. Still further, Heidegger helps set the question even if genealogical theology cannot be satisfied with his answer.

In Heidegger's thought, *Dasein* (the being – *sein* – who is there – *Da* – in the world), the being for whom being is a question, is the opening to "being there" (presence) in the world. *Dasein* has its facticity in this very condition: it is always with the world, and the world is always the presupposition to the question of *Dasein* as an opening to being. Heidegger examines the everyday structure of *Dasein* in a phenomenological analysis of being, and he does so because everyday life is exactly the peculiar manner in which *Dasein* finds itself in human form: it awakens as that which is thrown into the world. Yet the world too can alienate *Dasein* from its being, for the world as such is the system of the "they," as Heidegger says. "They" is the system of custom or habit where *Dasein*, by the sheer boredom of repetition, can forget its authentic self as the opening to the question of being.

In later writings, Heidegger recasts authenticity in terms of dwelling. He tries to link the very word "building" to "dwelling" by means of the old German word *buan*, which is the Germanic root of both building and being. Thus authentic building is dwelling – it is space that receives its sense of place in and through the manner of the building – while inauthentic building is akin to the technical use of space without a sense of place or being-with, that is, without the sense of "dwelling." "The essence of building is letting dwell,"[21] Heidegger says, but the real difficulty of the modern world is the detachment of these two words, these two senses, where technical building no

21 Heidegger, *Basic Writings*, 337.

longer addresses the need of humanity to dwell. In effect, technology alienates the question of being from humanity; it creates the anti-human being.

Insofar as genealogical theology means by presence the theological challenge to dwell in an archive, it is about being present in a certain resolute way. But in genealogical theology the sense of dwelling does not give itself over to the Heideggerian question of authenticity. Inasmuch as archaeological theology "displays" because it is empti-ness, genealogical theology dwells because it is aimless. But this "dwelling" is not Heidegger's dwelling. Genealogical theology knows that archive strategies create dwelling; therefore, there can be no div-ision between authentic and inauthentic dwelling. All dwelling is in-evitably constructed because it is inevitably an archive location. Dwelling is necessarily socio-political as a teleological product com-posed in forces. One cannot simply be in or with "dwelling," in the Heideggerian sense, without at once being in and with strategy. In other words, Heidegger does not grasp the epistemological priority in his effort to wait upon the question of being. He seeks the essence of words – their "*aletheia*" or uncovering or revelation – but does not consequently question the strategy used to uncover. Yet, is it not real-ly the question of strategy rather than "being" that Heidegger invokes when he raises the problem of language and being? *Buan* may ex-press a specific sense of building, but it does so as an archive event. Heidegger fails this political litmus test: he longs for the innocence of language as radical being without admitting that this question is fic-tion. He offers a "resolution" without understanding the archive; his "building" is a house of strategy no matter which reference point he regards as primal (that is, the old German or ancient Greek world).

When it is said that genealogical theology is aimless or has no pur-pose, this cannot mean that it is ignorant of strategy. Strategy is the substance of an archive's activity. Every event emerges as the expres-sive forms of force. Yet, it does not follow that the only option in the face of constant productivity is hopeless resignation. Rather, in op-position to the strategy of an archive there is counter-strategy, which Foucault understood as transgression. It is possible to be in an ar-chive as "dwelling in transgression," and this "dwelling" is the dwell-ing of genealogy.

Genealogical theology, then, is the practice of transgression as dwelling. Yet, as irony marked archaeological theology, so does it mark a theologian committed to genealogy. Genealogical theology is necessarily a posteriori or after the fact of being in the archive. It can be only through the affirmation of the location it already holds. Thus, while the normal tradition casts the weight of its credibility on a Platonic a priori, seeking as it does an ontological and pre-thematic foundation, genealogical theology moves forward with the acknowledgment of the accumulative forces of the archive and the fact that its status is one of a product. "Dwelling in transgression" is ironic dwelling because it is conscious of that which necessarily accounts for the moment of dwelling.

These subtle distinctions may not easily yield their meaning, but they can be approached if it is understood initially that genealogical theology is aimless. Aimlessness implies liberation from the teleological resolution, which may be the first point of reference in this new theology; second, aimlessness implies transgression because teleology is the archive's "aiming" and transgression is the archive's counter-activity.

At this point, two words of caution are in order. Liberation is a difficult word to employ in relation to genealogical theology. It is not suggested that genealogical theology escapes the condition of dwelling in the archive but only that it grasps dwelling with transgression. So, the liberation of genealogical theology is not freedom from constraint but freedom toward the event. There is freedom to engage the event with the "awareness of the event" gained in the work of archaeological theology. Liberation is a movement to the side of the event or, as described earlier, directed to the non-event. Genealogical theology, then, is called "aimless" because it is non-teleological: it is the act of liberated transgression that dwells without purpose.

A second word of caution is to resist associating transgression with deviancy, violence, or lifestyles radically set against social behaviour. To Foucault none of these descriptors constitutes transgression. Rather, archive forces produce the norm against which marginal acts are measured. Deviancy, as an example, is a reading of a social act from the foundation of a current archive's normal productivity. It is therefore a sign not of the nature of the perpetrator but of the functioning of the archive statements. Thus Foucault can say, "for the past 150 years the proclamation of the failure of the prison has always been accompanied by its maintenance."[22] The prison is a norm of

22   Foucault, *Discipline and Punish*, 272.

punishment set in the panoptic archive in such a way that the question of the prison already includes (indeed is founded upon) the
teleological reasoning for prisons. In short, the product is at once the
measurement. This circularity is broken only when the product itself
is transgressed. As a practical example, if genealogical theology were
to address the question of the prison, it would do so aimlessly in the
sense that it will not admit to the teleological necessity for the prison
but rather seek to break the reasoning of the prison through a genealogical orientation to the non-event. In this sense, dwelling in transgression is awareness of being liberated to the non-event as a means of
dwelling in the archive without dwelling in its teleology. The practice
of genealogy is not, then, deviancy but resistance. It is resistance as
non-co-operation with the teleological strategy of the archive. It is
presence in the archive but absence from resolution the archive poses.

To adapt some of Foucault's language, for genealogical theology
the way of being present in the archive is counter-teleology. As
Foucault put it, "we must make allowance for the complex and unstable process whereby discourse can be both an instrument and an effect of power, but also a hindrance, a stumbling block, a point of
resistance and a starting point for an opposing strategy."[23]
Transgression is a point of resistance. It is specific activity in the archive without the justification of the active teleological project.
Deleuze, in an interview, expressed exactly this, experimenting with
a certain vision of statements understood as linguistic domains.
Deleuze imagined the word "machinistic" indicating, "it is as if a social space were covered by what we would have to call an abstract
machine."[24] Then he goes on to explain that "this abstract machine,
at a given moment, will break with the abstract machine of the preceding epochs – in other words, it will always be at the cutting edge
(*à la pointe*), thus ... It would be the machinic point of a group or a
given collectivity; it would indicate, within a group, and at a given moment, the maximum of deterritorialization as well as, and at the same
time, its power of innovation."[25] Moments and locations of transgression, and the basic orientation toward the non-event (the aimlessness), are indeed the "deterritorialization" of the archive *episteme*.

23 Foucault, *History of Sexuality*, 101.
24 Deleuze, "Dualism, Monism and Multiplicities," 93.
25 Ibid.

They are strangely contextual points of counter-context. They are machinic points of forming a differently oriented strategy.

Deleuze's comments help give some sense to the insistence that genealogical theology is not a form of apology, for it remains lost to or undirected by the teleological setting. Yet, again, it is so with an awareness of its own form of irony. It is not as if genealogical theology achieves liberation from the archive; it is only that it achieves a way of dwelling transgressively in the archive. This brings us back to the distinction drawn between Heidegger and Foucault. If it is from Heidegger that we take the cue of genealogical theology's presence in the archive as dwelling, then it is from Foucault that dwelling becomes political and presence in the archive moves from Heidegger's passive waiting to Foucault's active participation. Heidegger lacks the sociological acumen that defines the thought of Foucault. In *Discipline and Punish*, panopticism is presented as the social order that produces the teleological necessity of discipline and disciplinary forms such that, as Foucault could dramatically say, one could no longer distinguish between the prison and the hospital and the school.[26]

Archaeological and genealogical forms of theology are liberated from the naïveté of the dominant apologetic tradition since the analytical task of these theologies travels from displaying in the former to participation in the latter. In both cases, the disengagement of teleology brings forward a climate of emptiness and aimlessness, but this is no despairing conclusion. It is rather the task of awakening, that is, actively dwelling in the serious question of responsible human thinking. This responsibility taken into theology means that it is time for theology to be accountable for – if first it can ever admit that it produces – the God-form. It must take responsibility for the side effects it has posed for so long protectively in apologetic resolutions. This new task requires a new liberty that, beyond defensiveness, both displays the God-form archaeologically and dwells in the archive counter-teleologically.

"How refreshing," a Zen saying goes, "the whinny of a packhorse unloaded of everything": archaeology and genealogy are about taking the space liberated from apology and, in transgression, delivering that space to awareness that eludes the weight of resolution.

26 Foucault, *Discipline and Punish.*

Bibliography

Aarsleff, Hans. *From Locke to Saussure: Essays on the Study of Language and Intellectual History.* Minneapolis: University of Minnesota Press 1982

Adams, Hazard and Leroy Searle, eds. *Critical Theory since 1965.* Tallahassee: Florida State University Press 1986

Adams, James Luther. *Paul Tillich's Philosophy of Culture, Science, and Religion.* New York: Schocken Books 1970

Adamson, Walter L. *Hegemony and Revolution: Antonio Gramsci's Political and Cultural Theory.* Berkeley: University of California Press 1980

Adorno, Theodor W. *Negative Dialectics.* Translated by E.B. Ashton. New York: Continuum 1973

Allen, Diogenes. *Philosophy for Understanding Theology.* Atlanta: John Knox Press 1985

Altizer, Thomas J.J. *The Gospel of Christian Atheism.* Philadelphia: The Westminster Press 1966

– *Total Presence: The Language of Jesus and the Language of Today.* New York: The Seabury Press 1980

Altizer, Thomas and William Hamilton. *Radical Theology and the Death of God.* Indianapolis: Bobbs-Merrill Company, Inc. 1966

Arac, Jonathan, ed. *After Foucault: Humanistic Knowledge, Postmodern Challenges.* New Brunswick: Rutgers University Press 1988

Arato, Andrew and Eike Gebhardt, eds. *The Essential Frankfurt School Reader.* New York: Continuum 1992

Asad, Talal. *Genealogies of Religion: Discipline and Reasons of Power in Christianity and Islam.* Baltimore: Johns Hopkins University Press 1993

Augustine. *The City of God.* Translated by Henry Bettenson. New York: Penguin Books 1981

– *Confessions.* Translated by R.S. Pine-Coffin. New York: Penguin Books 1982

– *Enchiridion on Faith, Hope, and Love.* Edited with an introduction by Henry Paolucci. Chicago: Regnery Gateway 1961

Bachelard, Gaston. *The Poetics of Space.* Translated by Maria Jolas. New York: The Orion Press 1964

Bannet, Eve. *Structuralism and the Logic of Dissent: Barthes, Derrida, Foucault, Lacan.* London: MacMillan Press 1989

Barthes, Roland. *The Fashion System.* Translated by Matthew Ward and Richard Howard. Berkeley: University of California Press 1990

Bataille, George. *The Accursed Share.* Translated by Robert Hurley. 3 vols. New York: Zone Books 1991 and 1993

Baudrillard, Jean. *Forget Foucault.* New York: Semiotexte 1987

– *Seduction.* Translated by Brian Singer. Montreal: New World Perspectives 1990

Baum, Gregory. *Essays in Critical Theology.* Kansas City: Sheed & Ward 1994

Bauman, Zygmunt. *Postmodernity and Its Discontents.* New York: New York University Press 1997

Beer, Dan. *Michel Foucault: Form and Power.* Oxford: Legend 2002

Bellour, Raymond. "Toward Fiction." In *Michel Foucault Philosopher,* 148–56

Bentham, Jeremy. *The Works of Jeremy Bentham.* New York: Russell and Russell 1962

Bergson, Henri. *Matter and Memory.* Translated by N.M. Paul and W.S. Palmer. New York: Zone Books 1991

Bernauer, James William. "Confessions of the Soul: Foucault and Theological Culture." *Philosophy and Social Criticism* 31, nos. 5–6 (2005): 557–72

– *Michel Foucault's Force of Flight: Toward an Ethics for Thought.* Atlantic Highlands, NJ: Humanities Press International 1990

Bernauer, James William and Jeremy R. Carrette, eds. *Michel Foucault and Theology: The Politics of Religious Experience.* Burlington: Ashgate Publishing Company 2004

Best, Steven and Douglas Kellner. *Postmodern Theory: Critical Interrogations.* New York: The Guilford Press 1991

Bouretz, Pierre. "La question du pouvoir." *Magazine littéraire,* no. 325 (October 1994): 30–1

Boyne, Roy. *Foucault and Derrida: The Other Side of Reason.* London: Unwin Press 1990

Braudel, Fernand. *On History.* Translated by Sarah Matthews. Chicago: University of Chicago Press 1980

Brown, Peter. *Augustine of Hippo.* London: Faber and Faber 1967

Byrne, James M. "Foucault on Continuity: The Postmodern Challenge to Tradition." *Faith and Philosophy* 9, no. 3 (1992): 335–52

– *Religion and the Enlightenment.* Louisville: Westminster John Knox Press 1997

Canguilhem, Georges. *The Normal and the Pathological.* New York: Zone Books 1991

Caputo, John D. *The Prayers and Tears of Jacques Derrida.* Bloomington: Indiana University Press 1997
– *Radical Hermeneutics: Repetition, Deconstruction, and the Hermeneutic Project.* Bloomington: Indiana University Press 1987
Caputo, John and Mark Yount, eds. *Foucault and the Critique of Institutions.* University Park: The Pennsylvania State University Press 1993
Carrette, Jeremy. *Foucault and Religion: Spiritual Corporality and Political Spirituality.* London: Routledge 2000
– "Foucault, strategic knowledge and the study of religion: A response to McCutcheon, Fitzgerald, King, and Alles." *Culture and Religion* 2, no. 1 (2001): 127–40
Carrette, J.R., ed. *Religion and Culture.* New York: Routledge 1999
Cassirer, Ernst. *Kant's Life and Thought.* Translated by James Haden. New Haven: Yale University Press 1981
Cate, Curtis. *Friedrich Nietzsche.* Woodstock, NY: The Overlook Press 2002
Chidester, David. "Michel Foucault and the Study of Religion." *Religious Studies Review* 12, no. 1 (1986): 1–9
Connor, Steven. *Postmodernist Culture: An Introduction to Theories of the Contemporary.* London: Blackwell Publishers 1997
Copleston, Frederick. *Religion and the One: Philosophies East and West.* New York: Continuum 2002
Cupitt, Don. *Creation out of Nothing.* London: SCM Press 1990
– *The Great Questions of Life.* Santa Rosa: Polebridge Press 2005
– *Is Nothing Sacred? The Non-Realist Philosophy of Religion.* New York: Fordham University Press 2002
– *Life, Life.* Santa Rosa: Polebridge Press 2003
– *The Old Creed and the New.* London: SCM Press 2006
– *Radical Theology.* Santa Rosa: Polebridge Press 2006
– *Reforming Christianity.* Santa Rosa: Polebridge Press 2001
– *The Way to Happiness: A Theory of Religion.* Santa Rosa: Polebridge Press 2005
Davidson, Arnold I., ed. *Foucault and His Interlocutors.* Chicago: University of Chicago Press 1998
Davis, Charles. "Our Modern Identity: The Formation of the Self." *Modern Theology* 6, no. 2 (1990): 159–71
Dawkins, Richard. *The God Delusion.* New York: Houghton Mifflin Company 2006
Deleuze, Gilles. "Désir et plaisir." *Magazine littéraire*, no. 325 (Octobre 1994): 57–65
– *Difference and Repetition.* Translated by Paul Patton. New York: Columbia University Press 1994
– "Dualism, Monism and Multiplicities." *Contretemps* 2 (2001): 92–108

– *Foucault.* Translated by Seán Hand. Minneapolis: University of Minnesota Press 1986

Deleuze, Gilles and Félix Guattari. *A Thousand Plateaus: Capitalism and Schizophrenia.* Translated by Brian Massumi. Minneapolis: University of Minnesota Press 1987

Derrida, Jacques. *Of Gramatology.* Translated by Gayatri Chakravorty Spivak. Baltimore: Johns Hopkins University Press 1974

– *Writing and Difference.* Translated by Alan Bass. Chicago: University of Chicago Press 1978

Detweiler, Robert, ed. *Semeia 23: Derrida and Biblical Studies.* Philadelphia: Scholars Press 1982

Dosse, François. *The History of Structuralism.* 2 vols. Minneapolis: University of Minnesota Press 1997

Dreyfus, Hubert L. and Paul Rabinow. *Michel Foucault: Beyond Structuralism and Hermeneutics.* Chicago: University of Chicago Press 1983

Eribon, Didier. *Michel Foucault.* Paris: Flammarion 1989

Ewald, François. "A Power without an Exterior." In *Michel Foucault Philosopher,* 169–75

Feuerbach, Ludwig. *The Essence of Christianity.* Translated by George Eliot. New York: Harper and Row, Publishers 1957

Flynn, Bernard Charles. "Michel Foucault and the Husserlian Problematic of Transcendental Philosophy of History." *Philosophy Today* 22 (1978): 224–37

Flynn, Thomas. "Foucault and the Eclipse of Vision." In Levin, *Modernity and the Hegemony of Vision,* 273–86

– "Foucault's Mapping of History." In *The Cambridge Companion to Foucault.* Edited by Gary Cutting. Cambridge: Cambridge University Press 1994, 28–46.

"Partially Desacralized Spaces." *Faith and Philosophy* 10, no. 4 (1993): 143–56

– *Sartre, Foucault, and Historical Reason.* Chicago: University of Chicago Press 1997

Foucault, Michel. *Abnormal: Lectures at the Collège de France 1974–1975.* Translated by Graham Burchell. New York: Picador 2003

– *The Archaeology of Knowledge.* Translated by A.M. Sheridan Smith. New York: Routledge 1972

– *L'archéology du savoir.* Paris: Édition Gallimard 1969

– *The Birth of the Clinic.* Translated by A.M. Sheridan Smith. New York: Vintage Books 1975

– *The Care of the Self.* Vol. 3, *The History of Sexuality.* Translated by Robert Hurley. New York: Vintage Books 1988

– *Death and the Labyrinth.* Translated by Charles Ruas. New York: Doubleday and Company, Inc. 1986

- "Dialogue on Power" (Transcript of Michel Foucault with students in Los Angeles in 1976). Centre Michel Foucault, Paris (1988), Document 533
- *Discipline and Punish*. Translated by Alan Sheridan. New York: Vintage Books 1979
- *The Foucault Reader*. Edited by Paul Rabinow. New York: Pantheon Books 1984
- *The History of Sexuality: An Introduction*. Translated by Robert Hurley. New York: Vintage Books 1990
- *Language, Counter-Memory, Practice*. Edited by Donald F. Bouchard. New York: Cornell University Press 1977
- "Linguistique et sciences sociales." *Revue Tunisienne de Sciences Sociales* (1968): 248–55
- *Madness and Civilization*. Translated by Richard Howard. New York: Vintage Books 1988
- *Les Mots et les choses*. Paris: Éditions Gallimard 1966
- "Nietzsche, la généalogie, l'histoire." Vol. 2, *Dites et écrits*. Paris: Éditions Gallimard (1994): 136–56
- "Of Other Spaces." *Diacritics* 16, no. 1 (1987): 22–7
- *L'Ordre du discours*. Paris: Éditions Gallimard 1971
- *The Order of Things*. New York: Vintage Books 1973
- *Power*. Vol. 3, *Essential Works of Foucault, 1954–1984*. Edited by James D. Faubion. New York: The New Press 2000
- *Power/Knowledge: Selected Interviews and Other Writings 1972–1977*. Edited by Colin Gordon. New York: Pantheon Books 1980
- "Power and Sex: An Interview with Michel Foucault." *Telos* 32 (1977): 159–61
- "Qu'appelle-t-on punir? Entretien avec Michel Foucault." *Revue de l'Université de Bruxelles* (1984): 35–46
- *Remarks on Marx*. Translated by R. James Goldstein and James Cascaito. New York: Semiotext(e) 1991
- "Structuralism and Post-Structuralism: An Interview with Michel Foucault." *Telos* 55 (1983): 195–211
- *Surveiller et punir*. Paris: Éditions Gallimard 1975
- *Technologies of the Self*. Edited by Luther H. Martin et al. Amherst: University of Massachusetts Press 1988
- *The Use of Pleasure*. Vol. 2, *The History of Sexuality*. Translated by Robert Hurley. New York: Vintage Books 1990
- "What Is an Author?" In Adams and Searle, *Critical Theory since 1965*, 138–48

Frank, Manfred. "On Foucault's Concept of Discourse." In *Michel Foucault Philosopher*, 99–115

Funk, Robert W. *Honest to Jesus: Jesus for a New Millenium*. San Francisco: Harper Collins 1996

- *The Poetics of Biblical Narrative.* Sonoma: Polebridge Press 1988
Gadamer, Hans-Georg. *Truth and Method.* New York: Crossroads 1990
Geering, Lloyd. *Christian Faith at the Crossroads.* Santa Rosa: Polebridge Press
  2001
- *Christianity without God.* Santa Rosa: Polebridge Press 2002
Gillespie, Michael Allen. *Hegel, Heidegger, and the Ground of History.* Chicago:
  University of Chicago Press 1984
Glücksmann, André. "Michel Foucault's Nihilism." In *Michel Foucault
  Philosopher*, 336–9
Goldstein, Jan. *Foucault and the Writing of History.* Oxford: Basil Blackwell
  Ltd. 1994
Griffin, David Ray. "Religious Experience, Naturalism, and the Social
  Scientific Study of Religion." *Journal of the American Academy of Religion* 68,
  no. 1 (2000): 99–125
Griffin, David Ray et al., eds. *Varieties of Postmodern Theology.* New York: State
  University of New York Press 1989
Grondin, Jean. *Hans-Georg Gadamer: A Biography.* Translated by Joel
  Weinsheimer. New Haven: Yale University Press 2003
Gutting, Garry, ed. *The Cambridge Companion to Foucault.* Cambridge:
  Cambridge University Press 2005
Habermas, Jürgen. *The Theory of Communicative Action*, 2 vols. Translated by
  Thomas McCarthy. Boston: Beacon Press 1984 and 1987
Hamilton, William. *A Quest for the Post-Historical Jesus.* London: SCM Press
  1993
Hampson, Norman. *The Enlightenment.* New York: Penguin Books 1968
Hasumi, Shiguehiko. "Foucault et le XIXe siècle." *Magazine littéraire*,
  no. 325 (Octobre 1994): 24–9
Hegel, G.W.F. *The Phenomenology of Mind.* Translated by J.B. Baillie. New
  York: Harper and Row Publishers 1967
- *The Philosophy of History.* Translated by J. Sibree. New York: Dover
  Publications, Inc. 1956
- *The Philosophy of Right.* Translated by S.W. Dyde. Amherst: Prometheus
  Books 1996
Heidegger, Martin. *The Basic Problems of Phenomenology.* Translated by Albert
  Hofstadter. Indianapolis: Indiana University Press 1988
- *Basic Writings.* Edited by David Farrell Krell. New York: Harper and Row
  Publishers 1977
- *Being and Time.* Translated by John Macquarrie and Edward Robinson.
  New York: Harper and Row Publishers 1962
- "Building, Dwelling, Thinking." In *Basic Writings*, 323–39
- *Identity and Difference.* Translated by Joan Stambaugh. New York: Harper
  and Row Publishers 1969

- *Off the Beaten Track.* Translated by Julian Young and Kenneth Haynes. Cambridge: Cambridge University Press 2002
- *Pathmarks.* Edited by William McNeil. Cambridge: Cambridge University Press 1998
- *The Question Concerning Technology and Other Essays.* Translated by William Lovitt. New York: Harper and Row Publishers 1977
- *What Is Called Thinking?* Translated by J. Glenn Gray. New York: Harper and Row Publishers 1968
- *What Is a Thing?* Translated by Eugene T. Gendlin. Chicago: Henry Regnery Company 1967
Hollier, Denis. "The Word of God: I am Dead." In *Michel Foucault Philosopher*, 129–40
Hoy, David Couzens, ed. *Foucault: A Critical Reader.* London: Basil Blackwell Inc. 1986
Hume, David. *A Treatise of Human Nature.* New York: Penguin Books 1969
Husserl, Edmund. *The Crisis of European Sciences and Transcendental Phenomenology.* Translated by David Carr. Evanston: Northwestern University Press 1970
- *Ideas: General Introduction to Pure Phenomenology.* Translated by W.R. Boyce Gibson. London: Collier-Macmillan Ltd 1962
Hyman, Gavin, ed. *New Directions in Philosophical Theology: Essays in Honour of Don Cupitt.* Aldershot: Ashgate Publishing Limited 2004
Hyppolite, Jean. *Logic and Existence.* Translated by Leonard Lawlor and Amit Sen. New York: State University of New York Press 1997
Ijsseling, S. "Foucault with Heidegger." *Man and World* 19 (1986): 413–24
Irwin, Jones. "Heterodox Religion and Post-Atheism: Bataille/Klossowski/Foucault." *Minerva – An Internet Journal of Philosophy* 10 (2006): 215–44
Kant, Immanuel. *Critique of Practical Reason.* Translated by Thomas Kingsmill Abbott. New York: Dover Publications, Inc. 2004
- *Critique of Pure Reason.* Translated by F. Max Muller. New York: Anchor Books 1966
- *On History.* Translated by Lewis White Beck et al. Indianapolis: Bobbs-Merrill Educational Publishing 1963
Kantorowitz, Ernst H. *The King's Two Bodies: A Study in Medieval Political Theology.* Princeton: Princeton University Press 1957
Kauffmann, Walter. *Nietzsche: Philosopher, Psychologist, Antichrist.* Princeton: Princeton University Press 1974
Kierkegaard, Soren. *Stages of Life's Way.* Translated by Walter Lowrie. New York: Schocken Books 1971
King, Richard. "Foucault and the Study of Religion in a Post-Colonial Age." *Culture and Religion* 2, no.1 (2001): 113–20

Kolakowski, Leszek. *Modernity on Endless Trial.* Chicago: University of Chicago Press 1990

Küng, Hans. *Does God Exist?* Translated by Edward Quinn. New York: Vintage Books 1981

Kurzweil, Edith. *The Age of Structuralism: Lévi-Strauss to Foucault.* New York: Columbia University Press 1980

Lacan, Jacques. *The Four Fundamental Concepts of Psycho-Analysis.* Translated by Alan Sheridan. New York: W.W. Norton and Company 1978

– *Freud's Papers on Technique, 1953–1954.* Translated by John Forrester. New York: W.W. Norton 1988

Lalonde, Marc P. "Power/Knowledge and Liberation: Foucault as Parabolic Thinker." *Journal of the American Academy of Religion* 61, no. 1 (1993): 81–100

Leaves, Nigel. *The God Problem.* Santa Rosa: Polebridge Press 2006

– *Odyssey on the Sea of Faith: The Life and Writings of Don Cupitt.* Santa Rosa: Polebridge Press 2004

Lemert, Charles C. and Garth Gillan. *Michel Foucault: Social Theory and Transgression.* New York: Columbia University Press 1982

Léon, Antoine. *La Révolution française et l'éducation technique.* Paris: Société des études Robespierristes 1968

Lévi-Strauss, Claude. *Structural Anthropology.* Translated by Claire Jacobson and Brooke Grundfest Schoepf. New York: Basic Books 1963

Levin, David Michael, ed. *Modernity and the Hegemony of Vision.* Berkeley: University of California Press 1993

Levinas, Emmanuel. *Outside the Subject.* Translated by Michael B. Smith. Stanford: Stanford University Press 1994

– *The Theory of Intuition in Husserl's Phenomenology.* Translated by André Orianne. Evanston: Northwestern University Press 1995

Love, Nancy S. *Marx, Nietzsche, and Modernity.* New York: Columbia University 1986

Lyotard, Jean-François. *The Differend: Phrases in Dispute.* Translated by Georges Van Den Abbeele. Minneapolis: University of Minnesota Press 1988

Macey, David. *The Lives of Michel Foucault.* New York: Vintage 1993

Macquarrie, John. *Twentieth-Century Religious Thought.* London: SCM Press 1981

Maesschalck, Marc. "L'anti-science de M. Foucault face à la critique de J. Habermas." *Revue des Sciences philosophiques et théologiques* 74 (1990): 567–90

Mahon, Michael. *Foucault's Nietzschean Genealogy: Truth, Power, and the Subject.* New York: State University of New York Press 1992

Major-Poetzl, Pamela. *Michel Foucault's Archaeology of Western Culture.* Chapel Hill: University of North Carolina Press 1983

Marion, Jean-Luc. *God Without Being.* Translated by Thomas A. Carlson. Chicago: Chicago University Press 1991

May, Todd. *Between Genealogy and Epistemology: Psychology, Politics, and Knowledge in the Thought of Michel Foucault.* Pennsylvania: Pennsylvania University Press 1993

– *The Philosophy of Michel Foucault.* Montreal & Kingston: McGill-Queen's University Press 2006

McCall, Corey. "Autonomy, Religion, and Revolt in Foucault." *Journal of Philosophy and Scripture* 2, no.1 (2004): 7–14

McGushin, Edward F. *Foucault's Askesis: An Introduction to the Philosophical Life.* Evanston: Northwestern University Press 2007

McKelway, Alexander J. *The Systematic Theology of Paul Tillich.* New York: Dell Publishing Company 1964

McWhorter, Ladelle. "The Event of Truth: Foucault's Response to Structuralism." *Philosophy Today* (Summer 1994): 159–66

Megill, Allan. "Foucault, Structuralism, and the Ends of History." *Journal of Modern History* 51 (1979): 451–503

– *Prophets of Extremity: Nietzsche, Heidegger, Foucault, Derrida.* Berkeley: University of California Press 1985

Mellor, Philip. "The Application of the Theories of Michel Foucault to Problems in the Study of Religion." *Theology* 91 (1988): 484–93

Merleau-Ponty, M. *Phenomenology of Perception.* Translated by Colin Smith. London: Routledge and Kegan Paul 1981

Michel Foucault Philosopher. Translated by Timothy J. Armstrong. New York: Routledge 1992

Milchman, Alan and Alan Rosenberg. *Foucault and Heidegger: Critical Encounters.* Minneapolis: University of Minnesota Press 2003

Miller, James. *The Passion of Michel Foucault.* New York: Anchor Books 1994

Müller, Denis. "L'Accueil de l'autre et le souci de soi." *Revue de théologie et de philosophie* 123 (1991): 195–212

Murphy, Nancey. *Anglo-American Postmodernity: Philosophical Perspectives on Science, Religion, and Ethics.* Boulder: Westview Press 1997

Niebuhr, Reinhold. *The Nature and Destiny of Man.* 2 vols. New York: Charles Scribner and Sons 1964

Nietzsche, Friedrich. *Beyond Good and Evil.* Translated by R.J. Hollingdale. New York: Penguin Books 1978

– *Daybreak.* Translated by R.J. Hollingdale. Cambridge: Cambridge University Press 1982

– *The Gay Science.* Translated by Walter Kaufmann. New York: Vintage Books 1974

– *On the Genealogy of Morals.* Translated by Walter Kaufmann and R.J. Hollingdale. New York: Vintage Books 1989

- *Twilight of the Idols and The Anti-Christ.* Translated by R.J. Hollingdale.
  New York: Penguin Books 1968
- *The Will to Power.* Translated by Walter Kaufmann and R.J. Hollingdale.
  New York: Vintage Books 1968
Nealon, Jeffrey T. *Foucault beyond Foucault: Power and Its Intensifications since
  1984.* Stanford: Stanford University Press 2008.
Olkowski, Dorothea. *Gilles Deleuze and the Ruin of Representation.* Berkeley:
  University of California Press 1999
Paras, Eric. *Foucault: Beyond Power and Knowledge.* New York: Other Press 2006
Pasewark, Kyle A. *A Theology of Power: Being beyond Domination.* Minneapolis:
  Fortress Press 1993
Peirce, Charles Sanders. *Reasoning and the Logic of Things.* Cambridge:
  Harvard University Press 1992
Petit, Jacques-Guy. "Le philanthrope et la cité panoptique." In *Michel
  Foucault: Lire l'oeuvre.* Edited by Luce Giard. Grenoble: Éditions Jérôme
  Million 1992, 169–200
Pinkard, Terry. *Hegel: A Biography.* Cambridge: Cambridge University Press
  2000
Pinto, Henrique. *Foucault, Christianity and Interfaith Dialogue.* New York:
  Routledge 2003
Poster, Mark. *Critical Theory and Poststructuralism: In Search of a Context.*
  London: Cornell University Press 1989
- "Foucault, the Present and History." In *Michel Foucault Philosopher,* 303–16
Prado, C.G. *Starting with Foucault: An Introduction to Genealogy.* Boulder:
  Westview Press 1995
Rahner, Karl. *Foundations of the Christian Faith.* Translated by William V.
  Dych. New York: Crossroad 1986
Rajchman, John. *Michel Foucault: The Freedom of Philosophy.* New York:
  Columbia University Press 1985
Ransom, John S. *Foucault's Discipline: The Politics of Subjectivity.* Durham:
  Duke University Press 1997
Ricoeur, Paul. *Husserl: An Analysis of His Phenomenology.* Translated by
  Edward G. Ballard and Lester E. Embree. Evanston: Northwestern
  University Press 1967
Risebero, Bill. *The Story of Western Architecture.* Cambridge: MIT Press 1979
Sartre, Jean Paul. *Being and Nothingness.* Translated by Hazel E. Barnes. New
  York: Philosophical Library 1956
Saussure, Ferdinand de. *Cours de linguistique générale.* Paris: Payot 1985.
Schaff, Kory P. "Foucault and the Critical Tradition." *Humanities Studies* 25
  (2002): 323–32
Schleiermacher, Friedrich. *Der christliche Glaube 1821–1822.* Berlin: Walter
  de Gruyter and Co. 1984

Schuld, J. Joyce. *Foucault and Augustine: Reconsidering Power and Love.* Notre
   Dame: University of Notre Dame Press 2003
Seem, Mark. "Michel Foucault, *Surveiller et punir. Naissance de la prison.*" *Telos*
   19 (1976): 245–54
Sheridan, Alan. *Michel Foucault: The Will to Truth.* London: Routledge 1990
Sherwood, Yvonne and Kevin Hart, eds. *Derrida and Religion: Other
   Testaments.* New York: Routledge 2005
Shumway, David R. *Michel Foucault.* Boston: Twayne Publishers 1989
Silverman, Hugh J., ed. *Philosophy and Non-Philosophy since Merleau-Ponty.*
   New York: Routledge Press 1988
Stoler, Ann Laura. *Race and the Education of Desire: Foucault's* History of
   Sexuality *and the Colonial Order of Things.* Durham: Duke University Press
   1995
Strauss, David Friedrich. *The Old Faith and the New* (Originally published as
   Alte und der neue glaube, 1872). Translated by Mathilde Blind. New York:
   Prometheus Books 1997
Strenski, Ivan. "Religion, Power, and Final Foucault." *Journal of the American
   Academy of Religion* 66, no. 2 (1998): 345–67
Strozier, Robert M. *Foucault, Subjectivity, and Identity: Historical Constructions
   of Subject and Self.* Detroit: Wayne State University Press 2002
Taine, Hippolyte. *On Intelligence.* Translated by T.D. Haye. London: Reeve
   1871
Taylor, Charles. *Sources of the Self: The Making of the Modern Identity.*
   Cambridge: Harvard University Press 1989
Taylor, Mark C. *About Religion: Economies of Faith in Virtual Culture.* Chicago:
   University of Chicago Press 1999
Taylor, Mark, ed. *Deconstruction in Context: Literature and Philosophy.* Chicago:
   University of Chicago Press 1986
Thiele, Leslie Paul. *Timely Meditations: Martin Heidegger and Postmodern
   Politics.* Princeton: Princeton University Press 1995
Thomas, Owen C. "On Stepping Twice into the Same Church: Essence,
   Development, and Pluralism." *Anglican Theological Revue* 70, no. 4
   (1988): 293–307
Tillich, Paul. *Dynamics of Faith.* New York: Harper and Row Publishers 1957
– *A History of Christian Thought.* New York: Simon and Schuster 1968
– My *Search for Absolutes.* New York: Simon and Schuster 1967
– *Systematic Theology.* 3 vols. Chicago: University of Chicago Press 1951–1963
– *Theology of Culture.* London: Oxford University Press 1959
Van Buren, Paul. *The Secular Meaning of the Gospel.* New York: The
   Macmillan Company 1966
Visker, Rudi. *Michel Foucault: Genealogy as Critique.* Translated by Chris
   Turner. London: Verso 1995

Ward, Graham, ed. *The Blackwell Companion to Postmodern Theology.* Oxford: Blackwell Publishers 1997

— *The Postmodern God: A Theological Reader.* Oxford: Blackwell Publishers, Inc. 1997

White, Hayden. "Foucault Decoded: Notes from the Underground." *History and Theory* 12, no. 1 (1973): 23-54

Whitehead, Alfred. *Process and Reality.* New York: The Free Press 1978

Winquist, Charles E. *The Communion of Possibility.* Chico: The New Horizons Press 1975

— *Epiphanies of Darkness: Deconstruction in Theology.* Philadelphia: Fortress Press 1986.

— "Theology, Deconstruction, and Ritual Process." *Zygon* 18, no. 3 (1983): 295-309

Wittengenstein, Ludwig. *Philosophical Investigations.* Translated by G.E.M. Anscombe. Oxford: Basil Blackwell 1967

Index